The Paston Women: Selected Letters

Library of Medieval Women   ISSN 1369–9652

Series Editor: Jane Chance

The Library of Medieval Women aims to make available, in an English translation, significant works by, for, and about medieval women, from the age of the Church Fathers to the fifteenth century. The series encompasses many forms of writing, from poetry, visions, biography and autobiography, and letters, to sermons, treatises and encyclopedias; the subject matter is equally diverse: theology and mysticism, classical mythology, medicine and science, history, hagiography, and instructions for anchoresses. Each text is presented with an introduction setting the material in context, a guide to further reading, and an interpretive essay.

We welcome suggestions for future titles in the series. Proposals or queries may be sent directly to the editor or publisher at the addresses given below; all submissions will receive prompt and informed consideration.

Professor Jane Chance, Department of English, MS 30, Rice University, PO Box 1892, Houston, TX 77251–1892, USA. E-mail: jchance@rice.edu

Boydell & Brewer Limited, PO Box 9, Woodbridge, Suffolk, IP12 3DF, UK. E-mail: boydell@boydell.co.uk. Website: www.boydellandbrewer.com

Previously published titles in this series appear at the back of this book

The Paston Women: Selected Letters

Translated from the Middle English
with Introduction, Notes and Interpretive Essay

Diane Watt
University of Wales, Aberystwyth

D. S. BREWER

First published 2004
Transferred to digital printing
D.S. Brewer, Cambridge

ISBN 978 1 84384 024 4

D. S. Brewer is an imprint of Boydell & Brewer Ltd
PO Box 9, Woodbridge, Suffolk IP12 3DF, UK
and of Boydell & Brewer Inc.
668 Mt Hope Avenue, Rochester, NY 14620, USA
website: www.boydellandbrewer.com

A CiP catalogue record for this book is available
from the British Library

Library of Congress Catalog Card Number is available
upon request

This publication is printed on acid-free paper

Contents

Acknowledgements

I should like to thank Melanie Price for her help in the early stages of this project, and especially for her invaluable assistance with the production of a first draft of the translation of the letters. Patricia Watt, as always, has been a careful and critical reader of my work. I would also like to express my appreciation of the staff in the British Library, the National Library of Wales, and the University Library in Aberystwyth (especially at the Interlibrary Loan Desk), for their helpfulness and efficiency. Without the support of the English Department at the University of Wales, Aberystwyth, which granted me study leave in the first half of 2003, and without a generous grant from the University Research Fund, this project would have taken much longer to complete. I am extremely grateful to Jane Chance for her help and advice, and to Karen Cherewatuk for her perceptive criticisms and constructive suggestions, and for her continuing support in all things Paston. Caroline Palmer has, once again, shown herself to be an encouraging and sympathetic editor. This book is dedicated, with love and affection, to my nieces and nephews.

Preface

The base text of this translation is Norman Davis' *Paston Letters and Papers* in two volumes.[1] This is the standard complete edition which has replaced James Gairdner's six volume edition.[2] I have, however, also consulted the original letters in the British Library in London, and where I have questioned Davis' findings in his edition I have included an annotation to this effect.

The processes of selecting, editing, and translating letters such as these are by no means straightforward. The first difficulty lies in choosing which letters, and indeed letter writers, to include and, more problematically, which to leave out. The second problem is that, by focusing solely on the letters of some of the women of the family and their female associates, the volume provides the reader with only one half of a dialogue or a part of a larger conversation. Given this exclusive focus on letters by women (which I justify in the introduction), the fact that the women largely correspond with their male relatives and associates rather than their female ones exacerbates this situation. Furthermore, identifying the letter writers and the recipients can be far from straightforward. Unless otherwise stated, I have followed Davis. Nevertheless, it should be noted that there are problems with the very concept of the 'author' of a letter.[3] Laying aside for the time being questions surrounding the literacy of the Paston women and their reliance on secretaries and scribes (discussed below in the interpretive essay), a number of letters might nevertheless be thought of as collaborative. Letter writers often requested the help of others. Thus Margaret Paston's letter to her priest Sir James Gloys includes the instruction that he 'write a letter in my name to Walter [Margaret's son] considering you already know my intentions for

---

1   *The Paston Letters and Papers of the Fifteenth Century*, ed. Norman Davis, 2 vols. (Oxford, Clarendon Press, 1971 and 1976). Letters, documents and plates discussed here and in the introduction and interpretive essay that are not included in this volume are hereafter simply identified in parenthesis as Davis. They are identified by the letter number allocated in that edition (in which the letters, documents and plates are numbered consecutively through the two volumes). Translations of these letters and documents are my own.
2   *The Paston Letters, A.D. 1422–1509*, 6 vols. (London, Chatto and Windus, 1904).
3   Giles Constable, *Letters and Letter-Collections* (Turnhout, Brepols, 1976), pp.49–50.

him' (no. 69).[4] In this case, the actual letter to Walter either was not written, or more likely, was lost following Walter's premature death. Sometimes an individual sought permission to write a letter in someone else's name. Margaret's second son John Paston III wrote three such letters in women's names on matters relating to his own business. Writing to his mother on the subject of his marriage negotiations, John III sketched out a rough draft of what she might write on his behalf to Dame Elizabeth Brews (the mother of his future wife). He even specified that she should follow his wording, but have the letter copied 'in some other man's hand' (Davis, no. 378). He then followed this with a draft of a letter on the same matter to be sent by his mother to himself, that he could then present to the Brews family in order to strengthen his own position. The third example is linked to John III's disputes with his father's brother. According to the endorsement of the letter, this is a copy of an original written by his father's sister Elizabeth Browne (Davis, no. 388). It is, nevertheless, more likely (as Davis suggests) that John III wrote a letter as if it were from his aunt, with the expectation that she would either copy it herself or have a fair copy made which she would then sign. Because, in these cases, we have enough contextual information (in the surrounding text and annotations, and in the nature of the corrections) for the attribution of the letters to John III rather than to the women to be uncontroversial, I have not included them in this volume. Nevertheless, it should be clear that just because individuals sign letters in their own names, we can not always be certain that they composed them. Furthermore, judgements based simply on style or content may prove deceptive. Here a single example will suffice: Thomas Kela, a servant of the Brews family, wrote a letter to John III on the subject of the latter's marriage (Davis, no. 792). This closely echoes the tenor and even the language of a contemporaneous letter to the same recipient on the same topic that Kela's mistress had dictated to him (no. 82). Letter writers and their scribes often spoke in the same voice.

However, perhaps the greatest difficulty is deciding how much information about the materiality of the letters to include. Like modern letters, the Paston letters are generally addressed and dated, but the letters that were sent were folded and sealed rather than enclosed in envelopes, and the addresses were usually written on the exposed back of the letters for the benefit of the bearers. The letters were most commonly dated according to religious festivals in the closing salutation. In the form they have come down to us, they sometimes include corrections by the sender or secretary or annotations by the recipient, or other parties. Some of the letters (mainly those written to people who

---

4   Parenthetical citations by number alone here and in the introduction and interpretive essay refer to translated letters and documents in this volume.

were not members of the family) are drafts of letters or file copies that were not dispatched in their present form. Even the form of delivery of the letter might be significant, as writers often entrusted additional details to bearers to convey in confidence to the recipients.

Most translators or modernizers of the letters do not include the addresses. I have decided to do so, because I consider the address to be an integral part of the letter. However, in order to make the letters more accessible to the modern reader, I have both included a calendar of saints' days and religious festivals in this volume and added the date of each letter in modern form in square brackets at its head. Unless otherwise stated, I have followed Norman Davis' dating of the letters. Davis provides full explanations in the head notes to each letter. Generally speaking, I have not included marginal annotations whether by sender or recipient, although Davis provides these in his textual apparatus. Handwriting is another integral part of the material reality of the medieval letter, all the more so perhaps in those letters dictated to scribes. Davis provides a full analysis of the scribes of the letters, with which, in the case of some of the women's letters, I do not always agree. Where this is the case, I have included an annotation to that effect. I also discuss the question of women's literacy and their use of scribes at greater length in the interpretive essay. Otherwise, in my annotations to the letters, I restrict myself to identifying only the more significant scribes.

Again like modern letters, medieval letters in the vernacular rely heavily on epistolary conventions, some derived from French formulae, especially at the beginning (the greeting and opening inquiries about health and well-being) and at the end (when the writers 'sign off').[5] It is virtually impossible to render these phrases literally. The letters are also written in a range of styles. The dominant style can be characterized as informal or 'colloquial' (in so far as it may seem to resemble but is not the same as informal spoken English) and pragmatic. However, certain letters adopt a more oratory, didactic tone, while others include phrases or passages which use formal legal language, or discuss in some detail, using quite technical vocabulary, issues relating to the running of the household and country estates. As far as possible I have tried to convey the sense, tone and register of these letters in Modern English, with minimal footnotes. I include in the glossary technical terms that recur in my translation of the letters. These terms largely involve

---

[5]   Davis, '*The Litera Troili and English Letters*', *Review of English Studies* n.s. 16 (1965), pp.233–44; Davis, 'Style and Stereotype in Early English Letters', *Leeds Studies in English*, n.s.1 (1967), pp.7–8; Malcolm Richardson, 'Women, Commerce, and Rhetoric in Medieval England' in *Listening to Their Voices: the Rhetorical Activities of Historical Women*, ed. Molly Meijer Wertheimer (Columbia, University of South Carolina Press, 1997), pp.137–38.

three issues: marriage, the nature of the legal system, and collecting money from lands.

Finally, it should be remembered that, like Middle-English spelling, medieval grammar, punctuation and paragraphing were not governed by modern rules. Inevitably, given that most, if not all, of the letters in this selection were dictated to scribes, a number of irregularities and ambiguities occur which were presumably not intended by the author. I have silently corrected these, and imposed a regular punctuation system and my own paragraphing.

Introduction
Three Generations of Women's Letters

The Importance of the Letters

The decision to translate a selection of letters by the Paston women requires little justification. There are very few women writers in Middle English whose names have come down to us. The anchoress and mystic Julian of Norwich (1342– before 1426) and the pious laywoman and visionary Margery Kempe (c.1373– after 1439) are the best known.[1] Dame Juliana Berners, to whom the late fifteenth century *Book of Hunting* was attributed, may or may not have actually existed.[2] Earlier authors, such as Marie de France or Clemence of Barking, both working in the late twelfth century, wrote in Anglo-Norman.[3] While the former is famous for her short romantic tales or *lais*, she also wrote a religious work, the *Purgatory of St Patrick*. Clemence of Barking composed lives of saints. In fact most writing by – and indeed *for* – women in the European Middle Ages was of a spiritual or devotional rather than self-consciously literary nature. The letters of the Paston women supply us with more names and more authentic secular texts. Indeed, Margaret Paston's letters constitute the largest surviving set of personal writings by one woman in Middle English. Crucially, the letters of the Paston women also facilitate our understanding of the circumstances of their composition and the events being described.

The Paston letters and papers of the fifteenth century comprise the first major collection of private correspondence and related documents in English. Margaret Paston's correspondence is pivotal to the collection as a

---

[1] Julian of Norwich, *Revelations of Divine Love and the Motherhood of God*, trans. Frances Beer (Cambridge, D.S. Brewer, 1998); *The Book of Margery Kempe: An Abridged Translation*, trans. Liz Herbert McAvoy (Cambridge, D.S. Brewer, 2003).

[2] For a discussion of Berners' existence and extracts of the text, see *Women's Writing in Middle English*, ed. Alexandra Barratt (London, Longman, 1992), pp.232–37.

[3] See, for example, *The Lais of Marie de France*, trans. Glyn S. Burgess and Keith Busby (Harmondsworth, Penguin, 1986), and *Virgin Lives and Holy Deaths: Two Exemplary Biographies for Anglo-Norman Women*, trans. Jocelyn Wogan-Browne and Glyn S. Burgess (London, Everyman, 1996).

whole. Margaret was clearly a keen correspondent, especially during times of family crisis. Colin Richmond points out that she wrote seventeen letters, many of them exceptionally long, in the eventful summer and early autumn of 1465.[4] What is more, as Richmond so evocatively puts it 'she wrote at any time and at all hours: on Sundays; on saints' days. . . .' Of the 421 documents written by members of the immediate family which have survived from this period (many more must have been destroyed and lost) 107 are by Margaret. Only three of these documents are not letters: an inventory of goods stolen from a Paston property; an indenture of lease; and a copy of her will (no. 75). The letters themselves are primarily addressed to her husband and, after his death, to her two eldest sons. Letters to three of Margaret's other correspondents survive: a letter to a cousin, either John Berney or William Yelverton (no. 56); one to the family chaplain, Sir James Gloys (no. 69), and a sole letter to a female correspondent, Dame Elizabeth Brews, mother of her future daughter-in-law, Margery (no. 73). There are several letters written to Margaret by her husband, a couple from one of her brothers-in-law; a considerable number from her eldest sons; a couple from her middle two sons; none from her youngest son nor from either of her daughters. Of the letters written to Margaret by individuals who were not of the immediate family, perhaps the most interesting are the two from other women, both relatives and friends. One is from Alice Crane (not included in this collection, but discussed in the interpretive essay; Davis, no. 711), the other from Elizabeth Clere (no. 79).

The second most prolific female correspondent was Margaret's mother-in-law Agnes Paston. Only twenty-two letters and papers are attributed to Agnes, including three indentures of lease, one indenture of marriage settlement, one memorandum (no. 12), and four versions of her will (extracts of three drafts appear as nos. 15–17 in this volume; in addition see Davis, no. 34). One letter is to her husband, one to her second son, and the rest are to her eldest son. There are only four letters to Agnes in the collection, three by non-family members. Two letters from Agnes' daughter Elizabeth survive (nos. 18–19), one written to Agnes herself, alongside Elizabeth's will (no. 20), and a draft letter apparently written in Elizabeth's name by one of her nephews for her to sign (Davis, no. 388). Unfortunately, no letters were written, or at least kept, from Margaret Paston's two daughters, Anne and Margery, although one to Margery from Richard Calle has been preserved (Davis, no. 861). Margery had married Richard Calle, a family servant, despite the opposition of her mother and brothers. This love letter was written soon

4   Colin Richmond, *The Paston Family in the Fifteenth Century: Endings* (Manchester, Manchester University Press, 2000), p.92.

after the momentous event. There are also six letters from Margery Brews Paston, two written to Margaret's second son while their marriage was still being negotiated, the others written to him in later years. One letter to Margery from her husband exists (Davis, no. 389).

In addition to the large number of letters and documents by women who either married into or were born into the main line of the Paston family, there are another thirty-six in the collection and related documents attributed to women. These correspondents are from a range of social backgrounds, including more distant kin (such as Alice Crane and Elizabeth Clere, mentioned above) and neighbours, as well as duchesses and countesses; there is even a letter from the Queen in the related documents. Amongst the main collection there is a letter from Joan Keteryche, Abbess of Denny (Davis, no. 656). Some of these letters appear in this volume. Of those that do not, a number are worthy of comment. These include a letter (Davis, no. 426) by Eleanor Chamber, the grandmother of Margaret, who, at the time when Eleanor wrote (in 1442), had only been married to a Paston for a couple of years, and a much later letter from Elizabeth Mundford, Margaret's maternal aunt (Davis, no. 657). There are also copies of the wills of the wives of two of Margaret's sons (Davis, nos. 929 and 930).[5] Amongst the family letters to other women who are not close kin are letters from Margaret's second son to potential marriage partners (Davis, no. 362 to 'Mistress Anne'; and Davis, no. 373 to an unknown lady).

Three generations of the Paston women are represented by this selection of translated letters. The principal of selection has been to provide a representative sample of the letters and papers written by women in the main family line, or with very close connections to it. Agnes represents the first generation: included are some of her letters, a memorandum of errands, and a series of extracts from her draft wills. The letters and part of the will of Agnes' daughter Elizabeth head the second generation. This is followed by a large number of Margaret's letters, and an extract from her will. Included next is a set of letters from two of the more significant female family connections to appear in the collection: Elizabeth Clere and Dame Elizabeth Brews. It is worth observing here that, with the possible exception of the Abbess of Denny (who was of course married to Christ and the head of her community of women), there are no letters from women we can accurately

---

[5] Davis does not include the will of Elizabeth Clere under the heading of 'related documents' in volume 2 of his edition. It is described by Colin Richmond in his essay 'Elizabeth Clere: Friend of the Pastons' in *Medieval Women: Texts and Contexts in Late Medieval Britain, Essays for Felicity Riddy*, ed. Jocelyn Wogan-Browne, Rosalynn Voaden, Arlyn Diamond, Ann Hutchison, Carol M. Meale and Lesley Johnson (Turnhout, Brepols, 2000), pp.265–72.

describe as single.[6] As Richmond observes, 'only when a woman was to become a man's wife or had become a man's widow, do we know anything about her, unless, that is, she had been his mistress'.[7] Solitary letters written by two mistresses of Margaret's eldest son (who died aged only thirty-seven and unmarried), Cecily Daune and Constance Reynyforth, lead us into the correspondence of the third generation. The second of these women was the mother of John II's daughter, also called Constance. The remaining letters are those by Margaret's daughter-in-law, Margery Brews Paston.

The Letter Writers and Their Lives

The first family matriarch was then Agnes Berry Paston (born c.1405), daughter of Sir Edmund Berry of Horwellbury, Hertfordshire. She married William Paston I, who was more than twenty-five years her senior, in 1420, and from his point of view, the match was a good one. His father Clement had been only a minor landowner, taking his name from the small coastal village where he dwelled. Together, Agnes and William were largely responsible for elevating the status of the Paston family. Agnes brought property into the marriage and, following her father's death, she inherited considerable wealth, including the manors of Horwellbury, Marlingford, and Stanstead. William I inherited land from his father and maternal uncle, and purchased considerably more. He was, by profession, a lawyer and in 1429 was appointed Judge of the Common Bench. Agnes and William I had four sons and one daughter. William I gave Agnes the manors of Oxnead and Paston for her life, and she spent some of her widowhood in these properties, but much of it in Norwich. Following the death of her husband in 1444, her relations with her eldest son became strained (nos. 14 and 16–17), although she continued to be on close terms with his wife. Her relations with her daughter Elizabeth were particularly fraught, at least until her marriage (nos. 31, 34, 76). In the last years of her life, Agnes moved to London to live with her third son, William II, who had married Lady Anne Beaufort, daughter of Edmund, Duke of Somerset. Agnes died in 1479, possibly from plague.

Agnes' daughter Elizabeth (born in 1429) caused her family considerable anxiety by failing for many years to secure herself a husband, and she

---

[6]   On the dearth of early letters by single women more generally, see the introduction to *Early Modern Women's Letter Writing, 1450–1700*, ed. James Daybell (Basingstoke, Palgrave, 2001), p.13.
[7]   Richmond, *Endings*, p.49.

suffered at the hands of her mother who at one stage kept her locked up and beat her regularly (no. 76). A series of at least four suitors were proposed by her relatives, including Sir Stephen Scrope, an unattractive man some thirty years her senior.[8] In the end her mother could not bear to keep her at home and she was sent into the service of Lady Pole in London (no. 12). However, she did eventually marry not once, but twice, first to Robert Poynings in 1458, who died in battle less than three years later, and then in 1471 to Sir George Browne (executed in 1483). In her widowhood she was exceptionally rich. She had one son by her first husband, and another son and a daughter by her second. She died in 1488.

Margaret Mautby was a gentlewoman from near Yarmouth. Her father was John Mautby of Mautby, in Norfolk, and her mother was Margery Berney Mautby. Margaret was born c.1420 at her mother's family home of Reedham. After the death of Margaret's father, her mother married Ralph Garneys, but Margaret's inheritance (she was her father's sole heir) remained intact. She married Agnes' eldest son, John I around 1440. Margaret was even wealthier than Agnes and also brought property with her. She was also well connected, and the social links forged by the wedding, namely her kinship through her mother's family to Scrope's stepfather, the wealthy soldier Sir John Fastolf, were to have a significant impact on the family's future.[9] John I had been educated at Trinity Hall and Peterhouse, Cambridge, and had studied law at the Inner Temple. In the 1450s he became Fastolf's chief advisor and confidant. Following Fastolf's death (which is alluded to in letter no. 36 in which Margaret discusses appropriate mourning etiquette) John I asserted his rights as his heir, taking possession of Fastolf's lands, including the manors at Caister and Hellesdon. John I spent much of his time in London, and indeed was imprisoned in the Fleet three times in the 1460s, where Margaret visited him in the last year of his life (nos. 52 and 53), and Margaret acted as his estate manager in his frequent absences. The letters written in these times convey information and news, request instructions for the running of the household and the land-holdings, and seek and offer advice.

Margaret and John I had seven children: five sons, and two daughters. Margaret's favourite appears to have been her second youngest son Walter

---

[8] On Scrope, see Jonathan Hughes, 'Stephen Scrope and the Circle of Sir John Fastolf: Moral and Intellectual Outlooks' in *Medieval Knighthood IV: Papers from the Fifth Strawberry Hill Conference 1990*, ed. Christopher Harper-Bill and Ruth Harvey (Woodbridge, Boydell Press, 1992), pp.109–46.

[9] Fastolf is one possible antecedent of Shakespeare's Falstaff: Hughes, 'Stephen Scrope', p.129.

(see no. 69). Her relationship with her eldest son, John II, was often strained, especially after John I's death in 1466.[10] The closeness of her relationship to her priest Sir James Gloys also intensified disagreements with her sons, especially her second and third sons, John III and Edmond (Davis, no. 353; see no. 65 in this volume). While Margaret spent a great deal of time in the company of her mother-in-law, her relations with her daughters also proved difficult. The elder, Margery, proved a disappointment to her family when she eschewed marriage to a social superior or equal, and, in 1469, became secretly betrothed to Richard Calle, the family bailiff. Despite staunch opposition from Agnes and Margaret she held her ground (no. 60). Margaret does not appear to have been reconciled with her, although Calle remained in the family's service and Margaret remembered the couple's children in her will (no. 75). The second daughter, Anne, also caused her mother some disquiet. Having been placed in the household of a relative, Sir William Calthorp, she was expelled and sent home (no. 63). Anne also fell in love with a family servant, John Pamping. On this occasion the family succeeded in breaking off the relationship and Pamping was dismissed (Davis, no. 282), and in 1477 Anne married William Yelverton, the grandson of a former friend and then opponent of her father, with their blessing. It is likely that, some twenty years after her marriage, Anne died in childbirth. When not residing at Caister or Hellesdon, Margaret lived mainly in Norwich. Around 1474, she moved back to her own family property at Mautby. She died in 1484.

Elizabeth Uvedale Clere of Ormesby was a cousin of the family. She married Robert in 1434 and the couple had three sons and a daughter.[11] Widowed in 1446, shortly after Agnes Paston, she was an intimate of both Agnes and Margaret, but closer in age to the latter. She helped the family in various business and domestic matters. For example, she attempted to intervene on Elizabeth Paston's behalf at the time of the negotiations with Stephen Scrope (no. 76). At one stage, one of Margaret's young sons seems to have been in her care (no. 79). Margaret even wondered if it might be possible to arrange a marriage between her daughter Anne and Elizabeth Clere's son (no. 63). In April 1453 Elizabeth Clere was present when Margaret of Anjou visited Norwich. She had to lend Margaret Paston

---

[10]   The practice of distinguishing the three John Pastons (the father and his two eldest sons) by number is a modern convention. H.S. Bennett directs us to other examples of brothers sharing the same Christian name in *The Pastons and Their England*, 2nd edn. (Cambridge, Cambridge University Press, 1932), p.13 n.4. Presumably the custom resulted from the need to preserve the family name in a period of high infant mortality.

[11]   For this short biography I am indebted to Richmond, 'Elizabeth Clere', pp.251–73.

a necklace for the event (no. 32). Although the Queen took her to one side and urged her to find herself another husband, Elizabeth did not remarry, but for some forty years remained on her own and in control of her estates. Having inherited her husband's property, Elizabeth evidently enjoyed her independence and wealth. A late letter from Margaret to John III relates how Elizabeth had lent Margaret a substantial sum of money that the latter found herself unable to repay (nos. 64 and 65). Elizabeth Clere was a major benefactor to Gonville Hall, Cambridge.[12] She died in 1493. The Paston and Clere families were eventually united when one of Margaret's granddaughters married Elizabeth's grandson. Dame Elizabeth Brews, second wife of Sir Thomas Brews of Topcroft, became closely involved with the family at the time of her daughter's engagement to John III. Her earlier letters are concerned with this event, and reveal the extent of the role played by the couple's mothers in bringing the marriage negotiations to a satisfactory conclusion (nos. 80–82; see also no. 73). Her later letters indicate that she turned to her son-in-law for help in property matters.

Cecily Daune and Constance Reynyforth were both mistresses of Margaret Paston's eldest son, John II (1442–1479). Beyond what the letters themselves reveal, not much is known about either of them. John II had been sent to the royal court in 1461 and was knighted in 1463. He lived mainly in London, and, although he never married, he became betrothed in 1469 to Anne Haute, a cousin of the Queen (nos. 58–59); the engagement was only terminated several years later (see no. 70). His only child, a daughter, was illegitimate, and so following his death the estate went to John III (1444–1504), despite opposition from his uncle William II. Margery Brews married John III in 1477. Unlike Agnes and Margaret, she was not an heiress, and financial impediments almost prevented the wedding taking place (see especially no. 88). Nevertheless, and despite John III's evident womanizing which continued right up until the time of their marriage, the couple seem to have been very happy together. Margery lived in Norwich and at Caister. John III was knighted in 1487. Margery died in 1495, and John III then married the twice-widowed Agnes Morley. The eldest son of Margery and John III had three children who survived into adulthood. Their first child died aged only four, and their second son, William IV, eventually inherited the family estates. It was their daughter, Elizabeth, who married into the Clere family. A granddaughter of Margery and John III became a nun at Barking Abbey.

---

[12] Mary C. Erler, *Women, Reading, and Piety in Late Medieval England* (Cambridge, Cambridge University Press, 2002), p.71.

The Letters in Context

> I greet you warmly, and send you God's blessing and mine, requesting you to send me word how you are getting on in your business, because it seems a very long time since I heard news from you. And I advise you always to be careful to guard your important documents wisely, so that they do not fall into the hands of those who could do you harm in the future. Your father, may God absolve him, in his troubled period set greater store by his documents and deeds than he did by any of his moveable goods. Remember that if those were taken from you, you could never get any more that would be of such help to you as those are, etc. (no. 57).

So wrote Margaret Mautby Paston to her son John Paston II on 29 October 1466. For Margaret Paston, as for her husband and her sons, the letters written to and by family members, friends, acquaintances, patrons and servants may have been personal, but they were not entirely private documents, in so far as they were preserved as evidence for possible future disputes and court cases. At the same time, because of their very nature, for the most part the letters are not self-consciously literary pieces. (There are some exceptions to this rule.) On the whole, they are concerned with domestic and business matters. Their survival has to be understood to result from the swift rise to prominence of the Paston family in the fifteenth century in an age of political and social upheaval. As I have already suggested, Agnes Berry and Margaret Mautby played key roles: they brought into their marriages wealth and connections. Margery Brews did not. Although from a respectable family, she was only marrying a second son, and her father was unwilling to offer John II sufficient dowry. Fortunately, the intervention of Margaret Paston, who offered the couple the manor of Sparham, enabled the wedding to go ahead. On the whole, the women, and Margaret in particular, played an active part not only in expanding, maintaining and defending the manor houses and land, but also in placing their children in service and negotiating alliances for them. The mothers were pivotal in enabling their sons in particular to build up links at court and in the county. At the same time, however, both Agnes and Margaret were well provided for in their widowhoods, occupying several properties, at a time when the head of the family, John II, struggled to get by in London.[13]

---

[13] Richmond, *Endings*, p.79. Agnes' long life exacerbated the financial difficulties of her son John I. With the survival of both his grandmother and his mother, these problems were compounded for John II.

Yet it was not all plain sailing, and the women of the family suffered the vicissitudes of their fate as much as the men. In the mid–1440s a friar called John Hauteyn challenged Agnes' ownership of Oxnead manor (see no. 29). In the early 1450s Agnes became involved in a quarrel with her neighbours after she attempted to build a wall which would block a right of way. The half-built wall was pulled down (no. 7), and in one of her letters Agnes describes a heated argument which broke out in the churchyard following evensong (no. 8; see also no. 9). This episode is fairly typical and the women's letters illustrate the enormous amount of responsibility in economic and legal as well as domestic matters in the running of the household and estates. This was the case whether the women were widows working on their own behalves (see also the letters of Elizabeth Clere) or, as is the case with Margaret Paston, acting as custodians in the absence of husband and sons. For example, in 1448 Robert Hungerford, Lord Moleyns, laid claim to and then attacked the manor of Gresham, a property purchased many years earlier from Geoffrey Chaucer's son Thomas by William I, as part of his strategy of extending his estates. Agnes and Margaret found themselves insulted in the street – they were called 'flagrant whores' – while Gloys was physically assaulted (no. 25). Margaret tried to defend Gresham in her husband's absence – she instructed her husband to buy her siege provisions, including crossbows, axes and protective coats (no. 26) – but despite her resistance, she was forcibly evicted (Davis, no. 36). She then had to flee to Norwich, having heard of a plan to kidnap her (no. 28).

These traumatic events were only a presage of things to come. The conflict over the Fastolf inheritance arose because John I claimed that, before Fastolf died in 1459, he had, in a nuncupative or oral will, changed his bequest. According to the new will, John I was chief beneficiary in exchange for founding a college of priests and poor men and a relatively small sum of money (which, incidentally, was never paid). Although John I hastened to take possession of Caister and the other properties, he met with the resistance of the other executors, who included William Wainfleet, Bishop of Winchester, and William Yelverton I. They claimed John Paston I had exploited his position of trust in order to put forward a false claim. An extended legal battle followed and John I was imprisoned on a number of occasions. In 1465 the Duke of Suffolk sacked Drayton and attacked the manor house, village and church at Hellesdon, causing considerable destruction. Although not present during the assault on Hellesdon, Margaret Paston was again managing the household and the estates at the time, and she vividly describes the events and their after-effects to her husband (nos. 54 and 55).

It is worth noting that the figure behind the raids on the Paston properties was another woman, less scrupulous and even more formidable than Margaret: Alice Chaucer, dowager Duchess of Suffolk and granddaughter of the poet.[14] Margaret refers to her (not disparagingly) in one letter as 'my old lady' (no. 49). The pressure of the prolonged conflict took its toll on John I. He died only seven years after Fastolf at the relatively young age of 45, leaving his sons to carry on arguing the cause. 1469 was another dramatic year, when the Duke of Norfolk laid claim to Caister itself (he purchased it from one of the other executors) and, following a period of siege, with John III defending from within, took it by force. Margaret found herself in the position of transmitting news to John II, whom she reprimanded for risking the lives of his brother and family servants (nos. 61 and 62). Eventually the Pastons regained Caister, but lost most of the other property. Wainfleet incorporated Fastolf's college into Magdalene College, Cambridge, which he had recently founded. The dispute over Fastolf's will figures largely in the surviving correspondence. Many of Margaret's surviving letters relate either directly or indirectly to the conflicts which followed Fastolf's death.

Women's Letter Writing

The tradition of women's letter writing first emerged in the European Middle Ages.[15] In the early Middle Ages, the *ars dictaminis* or *ars dictandi*, in other words, studies in the art of letter writing, ensured that the formal requirements of epistolary composition were widely adhered to and the rhetorical criteria followed.[16] The eleventh and twelfth centuries have been described as the golden age of letter writing, even though most, but not all, of the authors in this tradition are male.[17] By far the most part of the surviving medieval women's letters are by religious women rather than laywomen. The correspondence between St Boniface (c.675–754) and his supporters in Anglo-Saxon England provide us with some of the

---

14   Richmond, *Endings*, p.7.
15   For a concise survey of women letter writers in Europe from Egeria in the early fifth century to Laura Cereta and Isabella d'Este in the Italian Renaissance, see the introduction to *Dear Sister: Medieval Women and the Epistolary Genre*, ed. Karen Cherewatuk and Ulrike Wiethaus (Philadelphia, University of Pennsylvania Press, 1993), pp.6–10. See also Eleanor Duckett, *Women and Their Letters in the Early Middle Ages* (Baltimore, Maryland, Barton-Gillet, 1965); Albrecht Classen, 'Female Epistolary Literature from Antiquity to the Present: An Introduction', *Studia Neophilologia* 60 (1988), pp.3–13; and Joan M. Ferrante, *To the Glory of Her Sex: Women's Roles in the Composition of Medieval Texts* (Bloomington, Indiana, Indiana University Press, 1997), pp.11–35.
16   See Martin Camargo, *Ars Dictaminis Ars Dictandi* (Turnhout, Brepols, 1991).
17   Giles Constable, *Letters and Letter-Collections* (Turnhout, Brepols, 1976), p.31.

earliest examples of letters by English women, mainly abbesses, plus three letters from an English nun who had travelled with Boniface to Germany.[18] We should not assume from this that the letters of religious women are necessarily similar in content or form. Notable examples of such letters include the correspondence of prophets and visionaries such as Hildegard of Bingen (1098–1179) and Catherine of Siena (1347–1380). The aristocratic abbess, Hildegard, an individual of exceptional learning and genius, composed highly rhetorical and self-consciously literary Latin epistles.[19] The illiterate Catherine, a member of the artisan rather than the upper class, dictated far more informal letters in the Italian vernacular.[20] The letters of the twelfth-century nun Héloïse (c.1100–1164) to her former lover and husband Abélard combine spiritual concerns with private anxieties and pain.[21]

The most famous secular woman letter writer of the Middle Ages is Christine de Pizan (c.1365–1431?). Also the first professional female author in France, she famously engaged in debates about women, their nature, history, and status. She championed their cause against the slanders of the writings of clerical anti-feminists, and, taking a humanist stance, argued for allowing women greater educational opportunities. Christine de Pizan was the author of a number of courtly verse epistles in French, including *The Epistle of the God of Love* and *The Epistle of Othea*.[22] She also composed a collection of polemical prose letters in the vernacular, which responded to and critiqued the *Roman de la Rose*.[23] Her *Book of the Three Virtues* includes a model letter

---

[18] Ferrante, *To the Glory of Her Sex*, pp.18, 26–27, and 31; and Laurie A. Finke, *Women's Writing in English: Medieval England* (London, Longman, 1999), p.113.

[19] See Gillian T.W. Ahlgren, 'Visions and Rhetorical Strategy in the Letters of Hildegard of Bingen' in *Dear Sister*, ed. Cherewatuk and Wiethaus, pp.46–63.

[20] See Karen Scott, ' "Io Catarina": Ecclesiastical Politics and Oral Culture in the Letters of Catherine of Siena' in *Dear Sister*, ed. Cherewatuk and Wiethaus, pp.87–121.

[21] See Glenda McLeod, ' "Wholly Guilty, Wholly Innocent": Self-Definition in Héloïse's Letters to Abélard' in *Dear Sister*, ed. Cherewatuk and Wiethaus, pp.64–86; *Listening to Heloise: The Voice of a Twelfth-Century Woman*, ed. Bonnie Wheeler (Basingstoke, Macmillan, 2000); and Constant J. Mews, *The Lost Love Letters of Heloise and Abelard: Perceptions of Dialogue in Twelfth-Century France*, with a translation by Neville Chiavaroli and Constant J. Mews (Basingstoke, Palgrave, 2001).

[22] *Christine de Pizan's Letter of Othea to Hector*, trans. Jane Chance (Cambridge, D.S. Brewer, 1990); *The Selected Writings of Christine de Pizan*, trans. Renate Blumenfeld-Kosinski and Kevin Brownless (New York, Norton, 1997).

[23] See Earl Jeffrey Richard, ' "Seulette a part" – The "Little Woman on the Sidelines" Takes Up Her Pen: The Letters of Christine de Pizan' in *Dear Sister*,

of advice from an older woman to a younger one. Like Hildegard and Héloïse, Christine 'mastered' and manipulated the rhetorical tradition of epistolary composition. There exists a link between Christine de Pizan and the Paston women. *The Epistle of Othea* was translated into English by Elizabeth's suitor, Stephen Scrope, who worked from a manuscript probably brought back by Fastolf following a military mission to France.[24] The Paston family owned Scrope's translation and the French poem was also included in a compilation manuscript commissioned by John Paston II.

With the rise of the vernacular, the later Middle Ages saw the emergence of the personal letter and the flourishing of the woman's letter in particular.[25] It is these developments which provide the most important context of the letters of the Paston women. The Pastons all, to varying degrees, followed and adapted letter writing etiquette and custom: like modern letters they observed convention. One Valentine letter written by Margery Brews to her fiancé John Paston III (no. 87), perhaps the most famous letter in the entire collection, is remarkable for its manipulation of epistolary formulae.[26] If the aesthetic and innovative aspects of women's letter writing should not be overlooked, nor should its potential as a means of empowerment. Karen Cherewatuk and Ulrike Wiethaus assert that 'through letters, women who desired to write could bypass the need for formal education, literary patronage, editors, and publishers'.[27] Even those letter writers who, like Margaret Paston, wrote from urgent necessity rather than with an eye to posterity, establish their authority through the pen.[28] The Paston letters can also be considered alongside other

ed. Cherewatuk and Wiethaus, pp.139–70; *Christine de Pizan and the Categories of Difference*, ed. Marilynn Desmond (Minneapolis, University of Minnesota Press, 1998); and Rosalind Brown-Grant, *Christine de Pizan and the Moral Defence of Women: Reading Beyond Gender* (Cambridge, Cambridge University Press, 1999).

24 See Stephen Viereck Gibbs, 'Christine de Pizan's *Epistre Othea* in England: the Manuscript Tradition of Stephen Scrope's Translation' in *Contexts and Continuities: Proceedings of the 4th International Colloquium on Christine de Pizan (Glasgow 21–27 July 2000)*, ed. Angus J. Kennedy with Rosalind Brown-Grant, James C. Laidlaw and Catherine M. Muller (Glasgow, University of Glasgow Press, 2002), vol. 2, pp.397–408; and Hughes, 'Stephen Scrope', pp.132–33. I am grateful to Jane Chance for pointing out to me this connection between Christine and the Pastons.

25 See Constable, *Letters and Letter-Collections*, p.40; Classen, 'Female Epistolary Literature', p.5; and *Dear Sisters*, ed. Cherewatuk and Wiethaus, p.12.

26 See Norman Davis, 'The *Litera Troili* and English Letters', *Review of English Studies*, n.s. 16 (1965), p.237.

27 *Dear Sister*, ed. Cherewatuk and Wiethaus, p.1.

28 See Diane Watt, ' "No Writing for Writing's Sake": The Language of Service and Household Rhetoric in the Letters of the Paston Women' in *Dear Sister*, ed. Cherewatuk and Wiethaus, pp.122–38.

medieval and early modern vernacular English collections such as the Stonor, Cely, Plumpton, and Lisle Letters.[29] Even though some of these collections only contain a very few letters by women, James Daybell estimates that some 10 000 women's letters from before 1642 have survived.[30]

Women's Writing in the Vernacular

A second important context for the Paston women's letters is the appearance of women's writing in the English vernacular in the late fourteenth century and throughout the fifteenth century.[31] This is a tradition that particularly flourished in East Anglia, although it was not, of course, exclusive to it. What is remarkable about this emerging tradition is that although it is associated with the production of mainly devotional texts, the authors were not, generally speaking, nuns.[32] One English woman writer of note of the fifteenth century was the anonymous author of *A Revelation Showed to a Holy Woman*.[33] This account of a series of dreams of purgatory that the writer had in August 1422 actually takes the form of a letter written by the visionary herself, a Winchester laywoman, to her confessor, John Forest. In the first half of the century, Dame Eleanor Hull (c.1394–1460), a wealthy widow, translated two meditative works, *The Seven Psalms* and *Meditations Upon the Seven Days of the Week*.[34]

---

[29] For the medieval collections, see John Taylor, 'Letters and Letter Collections in England, 1300–1420', *Nottingham Medieval Studies*, 24 (1980), pp.57–70; Watt, ' "No Writing" ', pp.136–37 n.3; and V.M. O'Mara, 'Female Scribal Ability and Scribal Activity in Late Medieval England: the Evidence?', *Leeds Studies in English* 27 (1996), pp.91–96 and 109–10. For a range of essays on later letters, see *Early Modern Women's Letter Writing*, ed. Daybell. Fascinating parallels also exist between the letters of the Paston women and the correspondence of two Czech sisters living in the same century, especially in the discussions of marriage and in the accounts of their daily experiences: see *The Letters of the Rožmberk Sisters: Noblewomen in Fifteenth-Century Bohemia*, trans. John M. Klassen, Eva Doležalová, and Lynn Szabo (Cambridge, D.S. Brewer, 2001).

[30] *Women's Letter Writing*, ed. Daybell, p.3.

[31] For an important recent study that locates the letters of Margaret Paston within this context, see Rebecca Krug, *Reading Families: Women's Literate Practice in Late Medieval England* (Ithaca, Cornell University Press, 2002), pp. 17–64. For an overview, see Finke, *Women's Writing*.

[32] An exception to this rule is the author of a collection of prayers called *The Faits and Passion of Our Lord Jesu Christ*, who may have been a sister of the Bridgettine house of Syon, which was founded by Henry V in 1415. See *Women's Writing*, ed. Barratt, pp.205–18.

[33] *Women's Writing*, ed. Barratt, pp.163–76.

[34] *Women's Writing*, ed. Barratt, pp.219–31.

At the beginning of the following century, Lady Margaret Beaufort, Countess of Richmond and Derby (1443–1509) translated part of Thomas à Kempis' *The Imitation of Christ* and also *The Mirror of Gold to the Sinful Soul.*[35]

However, as noted above, one of the earliest and most famous female writers in Middle English was Julian of Norwich. Julian took her name from the Church of St Julian in Norwich, where she became an anchoress sometime before 1413. Some forty years earlier, in May 1373, she had witnessed a series of visions during a period of severe illness. She wrote two accounts of her mystical experience, the Short and Long Texts. They are remarkable for their clarity and theological sophistication. While, as Beer puts it, the Short Text is more 'immediate and personal',[36] the Long Text includes a profound revelation of the Trinity, incorporating the master-servant parable and the famous discussion of Christ as mother.[37] Julian of Norwich was a contemporary of and acquainted with the other most well-known medieval woman writer in English: Margery Kempe, a married laywoman, mother of fourteen children.[38] Born in Lynn, Norfolk, she came from a family of similar social standing to the Pastons. Her father, John Burnham was five times Mayor of the town, and a Member of Parliament. Following the birth of her first child, she underwent a spiritual conversion, and eventually found her vocation as a holy woman, living in chastity and travelling on pilgrimages around England and abroad, journeying to the Holy Lands, Spain, and Germany. *The Book of Margery Kempe* is her account of her extraordinary life and visions. Kempe herself could not read or write, but dictated her narrative to a series of scribes, one of whom was responsible for the work in the form in which we now have it. *The Book* is

---

[35] *Women's Writing*, ed. Barratt, pp.301–10; see also Krug, *Reading Families*, pp. 65–113.

[36] Julian of Norwich, *Revelations of Divine Love*, trans. Beer, p.vii; and see Beer's discussion in the introduction and interpretive essay, pp.1–23 and 71–80.

[37] See M.L. delMaestro, 'Julian of Norwich: Parable of the Lord and the Servant – Radical Orthodoxy', *Mystics Quarterly* 14 (1988), pp.84–93; and Sarah McNamer, 'The Exploratory Image: God as Mother in Julian of Norwich's *Revelations of Divine Love*', *Mystics Quarterly* 15 (1989), pp.21–28. For a range of critical responses, see *Julian of Norwich: A Book of Essays*, ed. Sandra J. McEntire (New York, Garland, 1998).

[38] *The Book of Margery Kempe*, trans. McAvoy. Key recent studies include Karma Lochrie, *Margery Kempe and the Translations of the Flesh* (Philadelphia, University of Pennsylvania Press, 1991); *Margery Kempe: A Book of Essays*, ed. Sandra J. McEntire (New York, Garland, 1992); and Lynn Staley, *Margery Kempe's Dissenting Fictions* (Pennsylvania, Pennsylvania State University Press, 1994).

made up of two parts: the first and longer part was completed in 1436; the second shorter one was begun in 1438.

There are, manifestly, significant differences between these writers and the Pastons. Both Agnes and Margaret Paston appear to have been concerned with their own and their family's spiritual well-being, and both wrote letters of a religious exhortation to their sons (e.g. nos. 14 and 62). Yet, neither wrote primarily for spiritual reasons and neither wrote letters which could be described as devotional, far less mystical. Nevertheless, some parallels can still be drawn between Margery Kempe and Margaret Paston in particular. Both women took an active role in society: Kempe records that she set up her own milling and brewing business, which, however, failed; Margaret Paston was clearly successful at managing the household and the estates. What is more, both were willing to take on authoritative figures, both lay and clerical. Kempe took on figures such as the Bishop of Norwich (to whom she complained about the behaviour of one of the priests under his jurisdiction) and the Archbishop of Canterbury (whom she reprimanded for keeping an unruly household). Margaret Paston, with the help of her mother-in-law, was ready, if not to defy, at least to try to browbeat the Bishop of Norwich in the business of her daughter Margery's marriage (no. 60). The powerful authoritative voice of Kempe in *The Book of Margery Kempe* is echoed, at least to some extent, in that of Margaret Paston in her letters.

Conclusion

Dating from 1425 and continuing throughout the century, the Paston Letters offer an insight into the lives of three generations of a relatively prosperous Norfolk family. Written in the century of the Wars of the Roses, they reflect the lawlessness and unrest of the times. The letters of the Paston women are also revealing about the position and roles of women in late medieval society and give us a unique female perspective on the events of the time and on their own social, religious, legal, and even political lives. These are letters concerned with issues as diverse and fundamental as love and marriage, birth, illness and death, education and service, the household and the estates, legal disputes and court cases, and violence and fear in a period of war. As the interpretive essay will indicate, they are particularly enlightening about women's social history, especially female literacy, women's activities, and women's relationships, both within the family and with other women. However, the letters also can be analysed from a literary perspective as examples of women's writing. Both Agnes and Margaret Paston, for example, were fine story-tellers, and their letters demonstrate considerable range from a pragmatic plain style to a more ornate didactic and consolatory one. The letters of the Paston women are important as examples of female self-expression, but they also leave the reader in no doubt that both within the immediate context of the household and in the wider society of Norfolk, women could be important and influential figures.

Relationships between
the Female Correspondents and the Paston Family

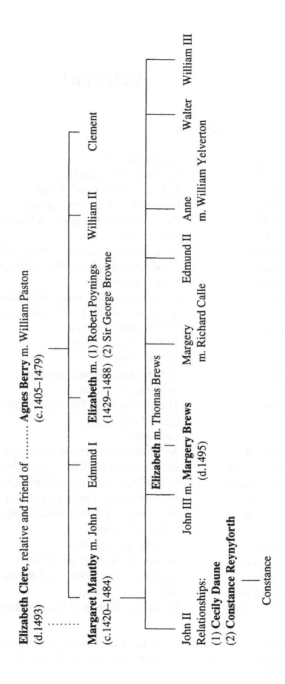

Elizabeth Clere, relative and friend of .... **Agnes Berry** m. William Paston
(d.1493)   (c.1405–1479)

Edmund I   **Elizabeth** m. (1) Robert Poynings   William II   Clement
           (1429–1488) (2) Sir George Browne

Margaret Mautby m. John I
(c.1420–1484)

Elizabeth m. Thomas Brews

John III m. **Margery Brews**
(d.1495)

John II
Relationships:
(1) **Cecily Daune**
(2) **Constance Reynyforth**

Margery   Edmund II   Anne   Walter   William III
m. Richard Calle   m. William Yelverton

Constance

Calendar[1]

Saints' Days and Festivals

5 January	Twelfth Night
6 January	Epiphany (Twelfth Day)
13 January	St Hilary, Bishop of Poitiers
25 January	Conversion of St Paul, apostle
2 February	Purification of the Blessed Virgin (Candlemas)
14 February	St Valentine, martyr
11 March	St Gregory the Great, Bishop of Rome
25 March	Annunciation of the Blessed Virgin
23 April	St George, martyr
3 May	Invention of the Cross (Holy Rood Day)
26 May	St Augustine, Archbishop of Canterbury
31 May	St Petronilla, martyr
11 June	St Barnabas, apostle
21 June	Midsummer Day
29 June	St Peter and St Paul, apostles
3 July	St Thomas, apostle
7 July	Translation of St Thomas, Archbishop of Canterbury, martyr
1 August	Lammas
15 August	Assumption of the Blessed Virgin
14 September	Exaltation of the Cross (also Holy Rood Day)
29 September	St Michael, archangel (Michaelmas)
6 October	St Faith (Foy), virgin and martyr
13 October	Translation of Edward the Confessor, King of England
18 October	St Luke, evangelist
28 October	St Simon and St Jude, apostles
1 November	All Saints or All Souls (Hallowmas)
6 November	St Leonard, hermit
11 November	St Martin, Bishop of Tours (Martinmas)

---

[1] This is not a complete calendar of saints' days, holy days and festivals, but a list of the most important religious feasts and of the days used to date the letters in this volume.

20 November	St Edmund, King of East Anglia
23 November	Clement I, pope and martyr
30 November	St Andrew, apostle
8 December	Conception of the Blessed Virgin
21 December	St Thomas, apostle
25 December	Nativity of Our Lord Jesus Christ (Christmas)

Moveable Feasts Dependent of the Date of Easter

Lent	Period of fasting, commemorating Christ's fast in the wilderness; forty weekdays before Easter
Ash Wednesday	First day of Lent
Palm Sunday	Commemorating Christ's entry into Jerusalem; Sunday before Easter
Good Friday	Commemorating Christ's crucifixion; Friday before Easter Day
Easter Day	Commemorating Christ's resurrection; occurs on the Sunday after the first full moon following the spring equinox on 21 March
Easter Monday	Monday following Easter Sunday
Rogation Day	Sunday before Ascension Day
Ascension Day	Holy Thursday, commemorating Christ's ascension; occurs ten days before Whitsunday
Whitsunday	Commemorating Pentecost; occurs on the seventh Sunday after Easter
Trinity Sunday	Sunday after Whitsunday
Corpus Christi Day	Thursday after Trinity Sunday

The Letters

The Letters

The Letters and Papers of Agnes Berry Paston

No. 1: Agnes Paston to William Paston I.

Agnes describes to her husband the introduction of their son, John I, to his future wife, Margaret Mautby. This letter is probably written in Agnes' own hand, thus the allusion at the end to the 'absence of a good secretary'.

[20 April, probably 1440]

To my honourable husband W. Paston may this letter be taken.

Dear husband, I commend myself to you, etc. Blessed be God, I send you good news of the coming and bringing home of the gentlewoman whom you know of, from Reedham, this very night, according to the agreement that you yourself made about it. And as for the first acquaintance between John Paston and the said gentlewomen, she welcomed him kindly and courteously, and said he was truly your son. And so I hope that no great negotiation shall be needed between them.

The parson of Stockton told me that if you would buy her a gown, her mother would add to it a fine fur. The gown is a necessity, and the colour should be a fine blue or else a bright sanguine.[1]

I entreat you to buy for me two gold threads.[2] Your fishponds are doing well.

May the Holy Trinity keep you. Written at Paston, in haste, the next Wednesday after *Deus qui errantibus*,[3] in the absence of a good secretary, etc. Yours, AGNES PASTON.

---

[1] Blood red.
[2] For hair decoration.
[3] The opening of the collect for the third Sunday after Easter.

No. 2: Agnes Paston to Edmond Paston I.

Agnes encourages her son Edmond, who is at Clifford's Inn, one of the Inns of Court in London, in his studies, and describes a conflict with the vicar of Paston over the boundary between the house and the church. She goes on to request building materials and to ask for news of the peace negotiations with France.

[4 February 1445]

To Edmond Paston of Clifford's Inn in London, may this letter be taken. To my well-beloved son,

I greet you warmly, and advise you to ruminate once a day on your father's advice to learn the law; because he said many times that whosoever would dwell at Paston would need to know how to defend himself.

The vicar of Paston, and your father, came to a firm agreement last Lent, and set boundary marks to show how broad the road would be. And now he [the vicar] has pulled up the marks and says he intends to make a ditch from the corner of his wall right across the road to the new ditch of the large close. And there is a man in Trunch called Palmer, who had from your father certain land in Trunch some seven or eight years ago in return for corn, and who truly has paid every year. And now he has allowed the corn to be seized in compensation for eight shillings of rent owed for Gimingham, which your father never paid. Geoffrey asked Palmer why the rent was not asked for in my husband's time, and Palmer said, because he was a great man, and a wise lawyer, and that was the reason men would not ask the rent of him. I send you, in a note enclosed in this letter, the names of the men who destroyed the pits in Ginny's Close.

I do not send you this letter to make you weary of Paston, because I live in hope, and you will find that they will be made weary of their work. Because in good faith, I am sure that it was your father's last wish to have done very well for that place, and I can show clear proof of that, though people would deny it.

May God make you a very good man, and send God's blessing and mine. Written in haste at Norwich the Thursday after Candlemas Day.

Find out from your brother John how many joists will suffice for the parlour and the chapel at Paston, and what length they need to be and what breadth and thickness they need to be. Because it was your father's wish, as I truly think, that they should be nine inches one way and nine the other way, and therefore arrange that they are squared[4] there and sent here, for

---

[4]   Cut into a rectangular cross section.

none of the kind can be had here in this region. And say to your brother John that it would be a good deed to remember Stanstead church. And I entreat you to send me news from beyond the sea, for here they are scared to repeat what has been reported.

By your mother, AGNES PASTON.

No. 3: Agnes Paston to John Paston I.

Agnes writes to her eldest son about the ultimately abortive marriage negotiations between her daughter Elizabeth and the elderly Stephen Scrope, ward of Sir John Fastolf.[5] Elizabeth Clere, who is referred to in this letter, also writes about this subject (no. 76).

[Not after 1449]

To John Paston may this letter be delivered.

Son, I greet you warmly with God's blessing and mine; and I let you know that my cousin Clere wrote to me that she had spoken with Scrope after he had been with me in Norwich, and told her what a welcome I had given him. And he said to her that he was pleased by the welcome I had given him. He conveyed to my cousin Clere that unless you gave him a warm welcome and words of encouragement at London, he would not speak further of the matter. My cousin Clere thinks it would be a folly to give him up unless you knew of another as good or better. And I have tested the opinion of your sister and I found her never so favourably disposed to any as she is to him, provided his land is clear as to title.

I sent you a letter by Braunton regarding silk, and regarding this matter, before my cousin Clere wrote to me, which was written on the next Wednesday after Midsummer Day. Sir Harry Inglose is very solicitous of Scrope for one of his daughters.

I beg you not to forget to bring me my money from Horwellbury when you come from London, either all or a large part. . . .

I can write no more, but may Almighty God be our good Lord, who always has you in his protection. Written at Oxnead in great haste on the next Saturday after Midsummer.

By your mother, A.P.

---

[5]   Fastolf was a professional soldier, who, having made his fortune at war, acquired extensive property in East Anglia, and built the large fortified residence of Caister for his own use. John Paston I became his confidant and advisor and was apparently named in his will as his chief beneficiary.

No. 4: Agnes Paston to John Paston I.

Agnes writes again to her eldest son concerning his sister's marriage. This time the prospective husband is a Sir William Oldhall.

[18 February, probably 1450]

May this letter be delivered to John Paston, dwelling in the Inner Temple in London, in haste.

I greet you warmly and let you know that today I was with my daughter,[6] your wife, and she was in good health at the time this letter was being composed, thanks be to God. And she informed your sister and me about a letter which you sent her, and that you have sought to persuade Sir William Oldhall to have your sister, and that, in the said letter, you request an answer in a short time about how she will be ruled in this business. Your sister commends herself to you, and thanks you with all her heart that you remember her, and keep her informed. And she entreats you that you will do the best you can to bring it to a good conclusion, because she says to me that she relies upon you to act according to both her honour and her advantage. And as for me, if you believe that his land is clear as to title, in so far as I perceive that your sister is well-disposed towards it, I consider myself very content.

And regarding the bond of the parson of Marlingford, which I sent you by John Newman, I entreat you to have it sued; and as for the parson and Lyndsey, they have come to an agreement.

And may God protect you, and send you His blessing and mine. Written in Norwich on Ash Wednesday.

By your mother, AGNES PASTON.

No. 5: Agnes Paston to John Paston I.

Agnes writes to her eldest son informing him that his wife, who is pregnant, is in good health, as are his children. She reports that enemy vessels have been causing trouble at the coast.

[11 March, probably 1450]

To John Paston, dwelling in the Inner Temple in London, may this letter be delivered in haste.

Son, I greet you warmly and send you God's blessing and mine; and as for my daughter, your wife, she is doing well, blessed be God, for a woman in her condition, as are all your sons and daughters. And because you will not send me any news, I send you such as there is in this region. Richard

---

6   'My daughter' can mean either biological daughter or daughter-in-law.

Lynsted came today from Paston, and informed me that last Saturday, Drawal, half-brother to Warren Harman, was seized by enemies when he was walking by the coast and they have taken him away with them. And they seized two pilgrims, a man and a woman, and they robbed the woman and let her go and they brought the man to the sea, and when they found out he was a pilgrim they gave him money and put him back on land again. And this week they have siezed four vessels from Winterton and Happisburgh, and Eccles' men are very afraid that more will be seized, because the enemies have ten large vessels. May God give us grace that the sea may be better protected than it is now, or else it will be dangerous dwelling by the sea coast.

I entreat you to greet your brothers warmly, and tell them I send them God's blessing and my own. And tell William that, if Jennett Lanton has not been paid for the crimson cors[7] for which Alison Crane[8] wrote to her in her own name, in order to procure it, that he then pay her and see that Alison Crane's name is struck out of her book. Because she says that she will ask no one for the money except Alison Crane.

And I entreat you that you will remember the last letter I sent you; and may God be with you. Written in Norwich on the Wednesday before St Gregory's Day.

By your mother, AGNES PASTON.

No. 6: Agnes Paston to John Paston I.

Agnes writes to her son about the dispute over the boundary with the church, and the building of a new road that prevents the religious processions. This dispute has escalated following the building of a wall. She also mentions, in passing, the ongoing need to sort out a marriage for Elizabeth.

[12 May, probably 1451]

To John Paston may this letter be delivered in haste.

I spoke today to a man from the Paston area, and he told me that a man from Paston told him that, on St Mark's day, Paston men were unable to go in procession farther than the churchyard, because the procession route was blocked off. And he said that people hoped that within a short time the wall would be broken down again.

---

[7]　Silk or other material woven into strips or a length of such silk used as a girdle or belt.

[8]　Alison or Alice Crane was a relative of the family. A letter from her to Margaret Paston survives.

Also, he said that I was fined for blocking the said route at the last general court, but he could not tell how much the fine was. And he who told me he asked the man who told him it if he had a copy of the fine in order to distrain for it. And he said no, but said that whoever would do it, would be more daring in taking it upon himself than he was.

Also, the same man told me that he met with a man from Blickling called Barker, who had lately come from London. And he told him that I had a lawsuit in London against Warren Harman of Paston, and said that Robert Branton was his attorney and said he saw him very busy on his behalf in London.

And do not forget your sister, and may God protect you. Written at Norwich on the twelfth day of May.

By your mother, A. PASTON.

No. 7: Agnes Paston to John Paston I.

Agnes tells her son that the wall has been demolished and that she has been fined for having it built.

[Probably 1451]

To Meye[9] Barker of the parish of St Clement in Norwich, to deliver to my master John Paston in haste.

On Thursday the wall was built a yard high; and for a long time before evening it rained so heavily that they were obliged to cover the wall and leave work, and the rain has fallen so heavily that it stands beneath the wall a foot deep in Ball's direction. And on Friday after the sacrament, someone came from the direction of the church, and pushed down everything that was on it and trod on the wall and broke some of it and went over it. But I do not yet know who it was.

And Warren King's wife, as she went over the style, she cursed Ball and said that he had given the road away, and so it turned out as John Paston said. And afterwards, King's people and others came and shouted at Agnes Ball, saying the same thing to her. Yesterday evening, when I ought to have gone to my bed the vicar said that, between mass and matins, Warren King and Warren Harman seized Sir Robert in the vestry and told him to say to me that truly the wall would come down again. And when the vicar told me I had not heard a word about it from Sir Robert, and still have not, because he says he is reluctant to cause any trouble. And when I came out of the church, Robert Eamond's revealed to me that I was fined sixpence last year

[9]   'Harry' scored out in the manuscript. 'Meye' (possibly meaning 'kinsman') is written above.

for a court suit, and he said it was twelve pence until Warren King and he got it down to sixpence. . . .

And may God be with you.

By AGNES PASTON, your mother.

No. 8: Agnes Paston to John Paston I.

Agnes reports that after a church service, she was cursed by her neighbours.

[8 November, probably 1451]

To John Paston, dwelling at the Temple in London, may this letter be delivered in haste.

I greet you warmly, and let you know that Warren Harman, on the Sunday after All Saint's Day after evensong, said openly in the churchyard that he knew for certain that if the wall were pulled down, even if he were a hundred miles from Paston, he knew for certain that I would say he did it and he would bear the blame, saying, 'Whatever anyone here says, even if it costs me twenty nobles,[10] it will be pulled down again.' And the wife of this Warren said in a loud voice, 'May all the devils of hell drag her soul to hell because of the road that she has made!'

And in the evening a certain person dined with me and told me that the patent only licensed me to close off one perch[11] in breadth, and that I had closed off more than the patent licensed, so people say. And John Marshall told me that there was a worthy woman came past the watering place and found the road blocked, and asked him who had blocked the road; and he said, 'they that had power to give it', and asked her what was more generous than a gift. And she said she had seen the day when Paston men would not have allowed that.

And may God be with you. Written at Paston on Monday after All Saints' Day.

By your mother, AGNES PASTON.

No. 9: Agnes Paston to John Paston I.

Agnes describes how on this occasion she was accosted in the church itself.

[21 November, probably 1451]

To John Paston, dwelling in the Temple in London, may this letter be delivered in haste.

---

[10] A gold coin worth 8 shillings and 6 pence.

[11] A measure corresponding to approximately five metres.

I greet you warmly, and let you know that on the Sunday before the Feast of St Edmund, after evensong, Agnes Ball came to me in my pew and wished me good evening, and Clement Spicer was with her. And I asked him what he wanted; and he asked me why I had blocked up the King's road. And I said to him I blocked no road except my own, and asked him why he had sold my land to John Ball; and he swore he had never reached an agreement with your father. And I told him that if his father had acted as he did, he would have been ashamed to have spoken as he spoke.

And all that time Warren Harman leaned over the partition and listened to what we said, and said that the change was a deplorable change, for the town was ruined by it and the worse off by £100. And I told him that it was discourteous to meddle himself in a matter unless he were called into a consultation. And walking proudly next to me in the church, he said that the blocking of the road would cost me 20 nobles, and still it must come down again. And I let him know that whoever pulled it down would pay for it. And he said that it was a good thing that I set men to work to collect money while I was here, but in the end I must lose my outlay. Then he asked me why I had taken his hay at Walsham, saying to me that he wished he had known about it when it was carried away, and he would have prevented it. And I told him it was my own land, and I would manage it as my own. And he told me to take four acres and go no further. And thus, presently, he left me in the churchyard.

And then I spoke to a certain person and asked him if he had heard anyone say why there was a dinner at Norfolk's house. And he told me that he had heard that certain people had sent to London to get a commission from Chancery to get the wall and the trench demolished again.

I received your letter by Robert Repps today after this letter was written thus far. I have read it but cannot give you more of an answer than I have written, except that the wife of Harman has the name of Our Lady, whose blessing and mine you have.

Written at Paston on the day after St Edmund's Day.

By your mother, AGNES PASTON.

No. 10: Agnes Paston to John Paston I.

Agnes writes about various property matters. She also expresses her concern that her two youngest sons have not been adequately provided for in their father's will. The letter ends with an allusion to the plague, which is rife in Norwich.

[16 November, probably 1452]

May this letter be delivered to John Paston, who is in London at the Inner Temple.

I greet you warmly, and send you God's blessing and mine; and regarding the business concerning which you requested my cousin Clere to write, she has done so, and I send you the copy enclosed in this letter.

As for the investigation, I have sent Pinchmore to seek information, and sent my own men to William Bacton and had them inquire in various places, and I have not heard anything from such inquiries. I do not know what it signifies. Robert Hill was at Paston this week, and the man who dwelled in Bower's place is out of there, and he said to Robert that he dare not abide there any longer because Warren Harman says to him that it is his place. . . .

Also, regarding Horwellbury, I send you a list of all the receipts since the death of your father, and written on the back a copy explaining how your father leased it to the said Gurney. I would like you to write to Gurney and order him to meet with you coming from London, and at least have him provide £10, because, according to my reckoning, last Michaelmas he owed, besides the debt to your father, £18 14s 8d.[12] If you will write to him to bring surety for both your father's debt and mine, and pay by the day, so that the man might give up and pay us, I will excuse £10 of the old arrears, and he can be made to pay 20 marks[13] a year. On that condition, I am willing to excuse him £10, and so it seems to me he should have reason to pray for your father and me, even if it was relinquished in my father's time. I understand from Robert that his wife is most unwilling to go from there; she says she would rather I should possess all her goods after her death than that they should go out of there.

Also, John Damme told me that Lady Boys will sell a residence called Hales, but he says she speaks about it secretly and says it is not entailed; as John Damme well knows, she has spoken as freely about other things that have not been so.

Also, he told me that he heard say that Sir John Fastolf has sold Hellesdon to Boleyn of London, and if it is so, it looks as if he will sell more. Because of this I entreat you, in so far as you have my love and my blessing, that you will help and apply yourself so that something can be purchased for your two brothers. I suppose that, if Sir John Fastolf were spoken to, he would be gladder to let his kinsmen have part than unrelated people. In my name, test him out about any such places that you consider to be most clear as to title. It is said in this region that my lord of Norfolk says that Sir John Fastolf has given him Caister, and will certainly have it. I send you a letter in Osbern's hand, which was the sheriff's, and John Damme's answer.

---

[12] Abbreviations for shillings and for pennies.
[13] Money of account: 1 mark is the equivalent of 13s 4d.

Also, bring my letter home to me with you, and my cousin Clere's copy of her letter, and the copy of the receipts of Horwellbury. And commend me to Lomnor,[14] and tell him that his best-beloved is in good health, but she has not yet come to Norwich, because people are still dying, but not so grievously as they did.

And God be with you. Written at Norwich in very great haste on the 16th day of November.

By your mother, AGNES PASTON.

No. 11: Agnes Paston to John Paston I.

Agnes sends news of two deaths.

[6 July 1453]

To my dearly beloved son John Paston.

Son, I greet you warmly and send you God's blessing and my own, and let you know that Robert Hill came home by Horwellbury; and Gurney told him that he had been to London for money, without success, and asked Robert that he should send me money by you. I entreat you not to forget it on your way home, and diligently to ask about another rent collector.

As for news, Philip Berney[15] passed to God last Monday in the greatest pain that I ever saw in a person. And on Tuesday Sir John Heveningham went to his church and heard three masses, and came home again never happier, and said to his wife that he would go into his garden to say a little prayer and then he would dine. And immediately he felt a loss of strength in his leg, and sank down. This was at 9 o'clock, and he was dead before noon.

My cousin Clere entreats you not to let anyone see her letter, which is sealed up under my seal.

I entreat you to pay your brother William for the four and a half ounces of silk that he paid for, which he sent me by William Taverner, and bring with you a quarter of an ounce exactly the same as that which I send you enclosed within this letter. And tell your brother William that his horse has farcy[16] and big running sores on his legs.

May God protect you. Written in great haste at Norwich on the eve of St Thomas's Day.

By your mother, A. PASTON.

---

[14] William Lomnor, a laywer who was a relative and agent of the Pastons.
[15] Margaret Paston's uncle.
[16] A disease of horses.

No. 12: Agnes Paston's Memorandum.

This is a list of tasks, presumably for one of Agnes' sons. Clement was a student at the Inns of Court. Elizabeth, still unmarried, had been placed in the service of Lady Pole.

[28 January 1458]

Errands to London for Agnes Paston, the 28th day of January, in the 36th year of King Harry VI.

To entreat Greenfield faithfully to send me word in writing of how Clement Paston has applied himself to his learning. And if he has not done well, and will not mend his ways, entreat him to whip him truly until he does mend his ways; and that is what the last master did, the best he ever had, at Cambridge. And tell Greenfield that if he will undertake to bring him into good conduct and learning, so that I may truly know that he applies himself, I will give him 10 marks for his effort; because I would rather he were fittingly buried than lost out of negligence.

Also, to see how many gowns Clement has; and those that are worn, have them brushed up. He has a short green gown and a short musterdevillers[17] gown that have never been brushed; and a short blue gown that has been brushed, and was made out of a long gown when I was last in London; and a long russet gown, furred with beaver, was made this time two years ago; and a long murrey[18] gown that was made this time twelve months ago.

Also, to have made for me six spoons, of eight ounce of troy[19] weight, well-made and double gilt.

And tell Elizabeth Paston that she must accustom herself to work willingly, as other gentlewomen do, and thus help herself somewhat. Also, to pay the Lady Pole 26s 8d for her board.

And if Greenfield has applied himself to Clement, or intends to apply himself, give him the noble.

No. 13: Agnes Paston to John Paston I.

Agnes writes to her eldest son about various legal matters.

[1 December 1461]

To John Paston in London, may this be delivered in haste.

I greet you warmly and let you know that today Bartholomew Ellis of Paston came to me in Norwich and showed me a rent roll for the term of

---

[17] A grey woollen cloth named after the town of Montivilliers in Normandy, where it was produced.
[18] Purple red.
[19] A standard system of weights used for precious metals.

St Michael in the 39th year of King Henry VI, and at the end of the said rent roll, in Warren King's hand, is written Agnes Paston 7d ob.[20] Also, the same Agnes for 5 acres of land, 20d.

Also, Alan Bayfeld asks the same rent for a year last Michaelmas.

Also, I am informed by an honest man that when the receiver Sharpe was last at Gimingham, Warren Harman was with him on various days, and reminded him that the fine for building the wall should be asked for again and distrained for.

Also, I sent you by Dr Aleyn's man the deed of rescue of Warren Harman and such names as Culling and Sammes put in of their own free will in the presence of John Northales, sheriff of Norwich, under their seals.

May God be with you and send you His blessing and my own. Written in Norwich on the Tuesday after the Feast of St Andrew.

Also, the said Bartholomew Ellis says that the said receiver would not take into account the rent in Trunch, nor the fines because of my court suit. Gunnor would not allow anyone to answer for me.

By your mother AGNES PASTON.

No. 14: Agnes Paston to John Paston I.

Agnes responds to her son's request for her forgiveness following a period of strained relations. Her letter is full of proverbial wisdom and biblical allusions.

[29 October, perhaps 1465]

To my dearly beloved son John Paston may this be delivered in haste.

Son, I greet you warmly and let you know that since your brother Clement tells me that you sincerely desire my blessing, may that blessing that I begged your father to give you the last day ever that he spoke and the blessing of all saints under heaven and mine come to you all days and times. And truthfully only believe that you have it, and you shall have it, provided that I find you kind and minded towards the well-being of your father's soul and for the welfare of your brothers.

By my advice, prepare yourself as much as you can to have less to do in the world. Your father said, 'In little work lies much rest.' This world is but a thoroughfare and full of woe;[21] and when we part from it, we take nothing

---

[20] Abbreviation for a halfpenny.
[21] Cf. *Knight's Tale* A.2847.

with us except our good and bad deeds. And no one knows how soon God will call him, and therefore it is good for every creature to be ready. Whom God chastises, him He loves.[22]

And as for your brothers, I know they will certainly work in your interest as much as they are able.

May Our Lord have you in His blessed care, body and soul. Written at Norwich on the 29th day of October.

By your mother, A.P.

No. 15: Agnes Paston's Will (Draft 1).

In the first surviving draft of her will Agnes claims that her husband had requested an oral addenda to his will. In this addenda, William Paston I had instructed Agnes that she should ensure that their younger sons were provided for after his death because he feared that they would not be provided for by his heir, John Paston I.

[16 September 1466]

To all to whom this present document must reach, I, Agnes Paston, until recently the wife of William Paston, Justice, send greeting in God everlasting, letting them know that I, the aforementioned Agnes, being of good and sound mind, on the 16th day of September in the 6th year of the reign of King Edward IV, and the year of our Lord 1466, make and order to be made my last will. . . .

And inasmuch as my husband, whose soul may God absolve, on many occasions, and especially, amongst others on the . . .[23] day of the month, recounted to me that the property which he had assigned to his two youngest, William and Clement, in his written will, was so little that they would not be able to live on it unless they should till the land themselves. And furthermore, saying that he had various other manors, that is to say the manors of Sporle, Swainsthorpe, and Beckham, the which manor of Beckham he intended to exchange for the manor of Palgrave if he was able to bring it about, then one of his two younger sons must have the said manors of Sporle and Beckham and no more, and the other youngest son must have all the rest. And the one who inherited the manor of Swainsthorpe should be under an obligation to the Prior of Norwich Abbey to pay a great sum of 4d every day in perpetuity to the monk who on that day sings the mass of the Holy Ghost in the Chapel of Our Lady in Norwich, where he

---

[22] Cf. 1 Timothy 6.7; Matthew 24.44; Hebrews 12.6.
[23] A blank space has been left to be filled in later.

intended to be buried, to sing and pray for his soul and mine and the souls to whom he and I are indebted or for whom we are bound in gratitude to pray.

And after that on the . . . day of the following . . ., my said husband, lying ill in bed, in the presence of John Paston (his son and mine), John Bacton, John Damme, and me, announced his intention concerning some of his children and me. At this time he assigned to the said John Paston's possession the manor of Gresham, and, after my decease, the reversion of such property as he gave me, asking him the question whether he did not consider himself content with this, speaking to him thus, 'Sir, if you will not do it, I will do it, because I am not willing to give so much to one that the rest shall have too little to live on.'

No. 16: Agnes Paston's Will: (Draft 2; fragment).

Agnes expands on William Paston I's intentions, giving more detail about the oral bequests he had made on his sickbed. This fragment is a very rough draft written on a scrap of paper, and it includes many corrections. Here we find further evidence of Agnes' literacy and of her legal competence.

[Probably 1466]

And after that on the . . . day of the month, my said husband, lying ill in bed, sent for me, John Paston, Bacton, and John of Damme to hear his will read out. And in our presence be began to read his will, and spoke first of me. And he assigned to me the manors of Paston, Latimer, and Shipden and Ropers in Cromer, for the duration of my life, and the manors of Marlingford, Stanstead, and Horwellbury, which were my own inheritance, and Oxnead, which was my jointure. And said, if he had given too little to anyone it was to me, because he had fared the better because of me, and he did so for none of the rest, except he had more to worry about which was mine as well as his. And then he read out John's share and assigned to him and to his wife the manor of Gresham, and after my decease, the manor of Oxnead; and he, understanding from John Paston's manner that he was not pleased because. . . .[24]

. . . Since out of sloth that his written will had not been made, but 'whatsoever may become of me, dame, I want you to know my intentions'. And he said that he wanted his two younger sons, William and Clement, to have such land as he had not included in his written will, and for his mass in perpetuity to come out of the income from Swainsthorpe. And he entreated

---

[24]   In the manuscript the sentence breaks off and the next paragraph is placed at right angles to the first.

me to report, record, and bear witness to this;[25] and he continued in this frame of mind and intention to assign his property thus until the day of his death. And I very freely venture to testify that this was his last will at the time of his death, which will, immediately after my husband's decease, I opened and declared to John Paston and all the other of my husband's executors, requesting them to see it carried out. And the said John Paston would not agree to this at all, asserting that by law the said manors ought to be his because my husband had not included them in his written will. And without my knowledge he obtained out of my possession the deeds and account of the fee of the said manors.

And after that the said John Paston took those of my husband's valuables that had been stored in Norwich Abbey by the said John Paston, John Bacton, John Damme and me, to be returned to all of us executors. And he took them and carried them away from the said abbey, without the knowledge of the Prior or that of any other person, and without the knowledge or consent of me or of any of our fellows. And he continues to keep it against my will and the wills of all of the other executors, without either restoring to the said William and Clement the aforementioned land or recompensing them for my husband's valuables or arranging the perpetual mass for my husband's soul according to his wishes. . . .[26]

No. 17: Agnes Paston's Will (Draft 3; fragment).

In this draft of her will, Agnes reveals more about John Paston I's unscrupulous behaviour following the death of his father. Unfortunately the manuscript is stained and unreadable in places.

[Probably 1466]

On the Thursday night before the Feast of the Assumption of Our Lady, between 11 and 12 o'clock, in the year of Our Lord 1444, the Sunday's letter being on the D,[27] my husband died, may God absolve his soul. And on the following Friday I sent for John Paston, William Bacton, and John Damme; and on the following Wednesday John Paston came, and on the Thursday,

---

[25] Referring either to oral or written testimony.

[26] Agnes goes on to make provision for William and Clement from the property which she inherited from her parents, and which had reverted to her under her husband's will, and to make provision for her husband's masses.

[27] Referring to the dominical letter, i.e. the letter designating the Sundays in a particular year (e.g. If the Sunday falls on the 1st of January, the letter is A, if it falls on the 4th of January, the letter is D).

John Damme and William Bacton. And on the Friday, John Paston, John Damme, and I went into Goodred's room and they asked me to show them the will. I let them see it, and John Damme read it. And when he had read it, John Paston walked up and down the room; John Damme and I knelt at the foot of the bed. The said John Damme asked me what my husband's intentions had been concerning Sporle, and I said that it was his intention that one of the two youngest sons should have it. He said privately to me that on his word he had said the same to him. Then at the same time I let them see the deed of gift, which I believe was confidential to all of those to whom this deed was made until I showed it to them. And they all swore accordingly, except John Paston and John Damme. After that my son John Paston never had any very kind words to say to me. And John Damme asked me which judge and colleague of his my husband trusted most, and I answered him to the best of my knowledge. . . .

After this, John Damme came and asked me which of the judges my husband trusted most, and said to me, 'Do you not remember a day when my master supported Marriott at Norwich?' I said, 'Yes, because I was there myself.' He said to me that my husband handed over to a certain man something written and sealed by my husband's hand, but he never knew what was in it.

The Letters and Papers of Elizabeth Paston Poynings or Browne

No. 18: Elizabeth Poynings to Agnes Paston.

After repeated efforts on the part of her family and friends to find her a husband, Elizabeth Paston married Sir Robert Poynings in 1458, when she was almost thirty. (For her marriage negotiations, see nos. 3, 4, 31, 34 and 76.) She wrote this letter to her mother shortly after the wedding. Relations between Elizabeth and her mother are evidently still strained, and Elizabeth asks for outstanding debts, undertaken on her behalf, to be repaid to her husband and to Lady Pole.

[3 January 1459]

To my very honourable mother Agnes Paston.

Very honourable and my most dearly beloved mother, in the most humble fashion I commend myself to your good motherhood,[28] beseeching you daily and nightly for your motherly blessing, wishing ever more to hear of your good health and prosperity, which I pray to God to continue and increase according to your heart's desire. And if it pleased your good motherhood to hear of me, and how I do, at the time that this letter was composed I was in good bodily health, thanks be to Jesus. And as for my master, my most loved one as you call him, and I should call him now, because I know of no reason to the contrary, and as I trust to Jesus never shall. Because he is very kind to me and is as solicitous as possible to make me certain of my jointure for which he is bound in a bond of £1000 to you, mother, and to my brother John, and to my brother William, and to Edmund Clere, who needed no such bond. Therefore I beseech you, good mother, as our most singular trust is in your good motherhood, that my master, my most loved one, should not be without the 100 marks at the beginning of this term, which was promised him on his marriage, with the remainder of the money left in my father's will. Because I have made a faithful promise to a gentleman called Bain, who was one of my most loved one's sureties, and was bound for him for £200, of which he demands to have £120 at the beginning of this term. And if he goes without this at this time he will claim the whole amount

---

[28] A term of address.

from us, which would be too great a loss for us. And he cannot pay off any of his other sureties without this said silver, and my brother John can tell you that well enough if it pleases him to do so.

And concerning all other things, as for my lady Pole, with whom I stayed, I hope that you will be my esteemed and good mother so that she can be paid for the expenses incurred for me before my marriage. . . .

And may Jesus, of his great mercy, protect you. Written in London on Wednesday the 3rd of January.

By your humble daughter, ELIZABETH POYNINGS.

No. 19: Elizabeth Poynings to John Paston II.

Following the death of Sir Robert Poynings in 1461 at the second Battle of St Albans, Elizabeth was dispossessed of her lands. Here she asks John Paston II to intervene.

[15 December, probably 1467]

To the honourable Sir John Paston, knight, may this be delivered in haste.

Honourable, and with all my heart dearly beloved nephew, I commend myself to you, wishing to hear of your prosperity and good health, which I entreat Almighty God to maintain and increase according to His Will and your heart's desire, thanking God for your improvement and health. Furthermore, informing you that Sir Robert Fiennes has done great damage in the estates which belonged to my husband and me in the county of Kent, in which William Keen and other people are enfeoffed, and greatly afflicts them and receives the produce and profits of a great part of them. And as for my said husband's estates in both the same county and other counties, over and above my jointure, my said husband, when he set off to St Albans' field, ordered his will to be made so that I would control all of his estates and those of Edward, his son and mine, and take the produce and profits of the said estates to pay for the keeping of his and my said son, to pay his debts and to protect the legal right of ownership and title of the same property. . . . In defiance of legal right and conscience, depriving me of my legal right and breaching my said husband's will, the said Robert Fiennes has caused a great amount of destruction and damage there, and for a long time has received the revenues and profits of the same, as a result of which I am deprived of my legal right and the said will cannot be carried out.

Therefore I entreat you with all my heart that you will canvass the King's Highness if it pleases him to address his honourable letters to be directed to the said Robert Fiennes, utterly forbidding him tenure, possession, and receipt of the revenues of the said manors of Tirlingham and others . . . so that

I and my assignees may occupy them in peace. And if any person should attempt to do the opposite, if it please the King's Highness, that a commandment might be given by him to the lord Chancellor to seal sufficient documents with his great seal to aid and assist me and my assignees in the same. And as for the manors of Easthall, Faukham, Ashe, and Chelsfield, with the rights appertaining to them, in the said county of Kent, which my husband possessed on his departure, and my son after until the time that the Earl of Kent, without any inquest or rightful title from the King, by colour of the King's letters patent took possession of them by force and turned him out of there. And now my lord of Essex has taken possession of them in the same method and way. If any redress for this can be obtained, I entreat you to attempt to obtain it.

And furthermore, I entreat you with all my heart that, should any general pardon be granted, that I may have one for John Dane my servant, whom the said Robert Fiennes has maliciously accused of felony; and that you discreetly try to achieve this and send me an answer in writing as quickly as you are able. As soon as it pleases you to send me part of the costs and expenses that you undertake and pay for the said legal actions, I will truly pay you back for the same, and, in addition to that, will reward you to your satisfaction, by the grace of Jesus, may He have you in His blessed protection.

Written in Southwark on the 15th of December,

By your aunt, ELIZABETH POYNINGS.

No. 20: Will.

Around about 1471, Elizabeth married her second husband, Sir George Browne. After being widowed a second time (Browne was executed in 1483 for taking part in Buckingham's revolt against Richard III), she became exceptionally wealthy, as her will testifies. No one in the Paston family is mentioned in the will.

[18 May 1487]

In *Dei nomine*, Amen.[29] On the 18th day of the month of May in the year of our Lord God 1487, and in the second year in the reign of King Henry VII, I, Dame Elizabeth, until recently wife of Sir George Brown, knight, being of sound mind and good memory, thanks be to Almighty God, make and order to be made this my present testament and last will in the manner and form following, that is to say:

First, I bequeath my soul to Almighty God, our Lady Saint Mary, and to all the holy company of heaven, and my body to be buried within the church

---

[29] 'In the name of the Father', i.e. the opening of the Lord's Prayer.

of the Black Friars in Ludgate, with my aforementioned husband Sir George; to which place I bequeath £21 for my said husband's soul and mine, our fathers' and mothers' souls, and for all Christian souls to be prayed for; and for 13 trentals[30] of Saint George to be recited and sung for us and them by the friars of the said place, in dirges[31] and masses along with other observances pertaining to the same in the following manner and form, that is to say: in the day or morning after my decease 7 trentals, and every week following until my month's-mind[32] one trental, and 3 trentals at my month's-mind in addition to the solemn dirge and masses which are required for me at that time. And I order my executors to see that this matter is carried out and performed, and also the said friars to take me from the place where I die to the said place already specified to be buried.

Also, I intend that, as soon as my body is buried and the expenses pertaining to that done and paid, that my executors provide and ensure that my debts be satisfied and paid.

Also, I bequeath to the vicar of Dorking church in the county of Surrey, for my aforementioned husband's soul and mine, our fathers' and mothers', and for all the souls to which we are obliged, to be prayed for in the year after my death, in dirges and masses to be recited or sung by him or his deputy, and to be remembered especially for one whole year, 20s.

Also, I bequeath to the repair of the aforementioned Dorking church, 20s.

Also, I bequeath to the parson of Saint Albans in Wood Street in London, for dirges or masses to be recited or sung by him or his deputy, in the same way as the vicar of Dorking is already commanded, 20s.

Also, I bequeath to the repair of the steeple of the said church of Saint Albans 20 shillings.

Also, I bequeath to the prisoners of Newgate, Ludgate, King's Bench, and Marshalsea, to each of those places, to be prayed for, 20d.

Also, I bequeath to bedridden people and other poor householders, both men and women, living in London and beyond in the suburbs of the same, and especially those who have known me and I them, 40s, according to the discretion and advice of my executors.

Furthermore, I give and bequeath to my daughter Mary, to further her marriage, all my plate[33] and other jewels, with all my entire adornments and all my household goods in my dwelling place or any other within the city of London or suburbs of the same, that is to say. . . .[34]

---

[30] Each trental was a series of 30 requiem masses.
[31] Funeral songs.
[32] A memorial service performed a month after the death.
[33] Household utensils in gold and silver.
[34] An enormous list of valuable possessions follows.

On condition that my executors, on the advice of my legal overseers, always order and keep in safe custody, to be held after my decease in a certain house of religion until the day of my said daughter's marriage, and to the furtherance and encouragement of the same, all and every part of the aforementioned plate and jewels, along with all the other household goods given and bequeathed by me to her as is written above, except such goods which cannot be protected from moths, which I intend her to have control and management of for the safety of the same and for her benefit.

And if my said daughter Mary should die unmarried, then I give and bequeath all the aforementioned plate, along with all the other household possessions, to my son Matthew, her brother. And if it should happen that he die unmarried, God forbid, then I give and bequeath all my aforementioned plate, jewels and household goods, in its entirety, to my son Sir Edward Poynings. And, if it should happen that the said Edward should die, may God protect us, then the aforementioned jewels and other goods listed above, with the exception of a plain standing cup[35] of silver and gilt with the cover, the knob and device of the same material, with a griffin's head at the bottom contrived on blue azure, weighing 26 ounces, which I give to my daughter-in-law Dame Isabel Poynings, is to be divided according to the advice of the overseers of this present last will and testament, and to be evenly shared between Anthony Browne and Robert Browne, my brothers-in-law, for them to do with it what they wish. And as regards my Agnus,[36] tablets[37] with diamonds, sapphires, large and small pearls, crosses, girdles, demiceints,[38] gowns, and all other things pertaining to my adornments, as listed above, if it should happen that my said daughter Mary should die, I give and bequeath all of it in its entirety to my kinswoman Margaret Hasslake. And if the said Margaret should die, then all the said adornments specifically listed above pass to my said daughter-in-law Dame Isabel Poynings.

Also, 20 marks, which I lent to my son Sir Edward Poynings, I intend it to be distributed at the discretion of my executors and overseers among those who are known to be my servants at the time of my death.

The residue of all of my personal possessions, chattels, and jewels, after my debts have been paid and my bequests carried out and fulfilled, and my funeral is over, I give and bequeath in their entirety to my sons Sir Edward Poynings and Matthew Browne, for them to deal with and do with as they wish, so that they pray and do for my soul as they would wish me to do for them, as they will answer before God.

---

[35] A cup with a foot or base.
[36] Figure of a lamb, emblematic of Christ. From *agnus dei*.
[37] Jewellery with at least one flat surface, or the flat setting in a piece of jewellery.
[38] A girdle of metal scales.

And I make and ordain to be made the executors of this my last will and testament my aforementioned sons Sir Edward Poynings and Matthew Browne, and their supervisors Humfrey Conisby and Richard Tuke. And I bequeath to each of my executors in return for their labour 110s and to each of my overseers for their labour 90s.

In witness hereof, I, the said Dame Elizabeth, have put my seal to this my last will and testament. Issued at London on the day and month stated above. . . .

The Letters and Papers of Margaret Mautby Paston

No. 21: Margaret Paston to John Paston I.

Margaret Mautby married John Paston I around 1440. A year later she wrote to him, when she was expecting her first child. In addition to the request for cloth for a new gown, this letter makes a number of indirect – and in the first case, ironic – allusions to Margaret's pregnancy.

[14 December, probably 1441]

To my most respected and honourable husband John Paston.

Most respected and honourable husband, I commend myself to you, wishing with all my heart to hear of your health and happiness, thanking you for the token that you sent me by Edmund Peres, entreating you to know that my mother[39] sent to my father in London for some musterdevillers[40] to make into a gown for me. And he told my mother and me when he came home that he ordered you to buy it after he left London. I entreat you, if it has not been bought, that you undertake to buy it and send it home as soon as you can. Because I have no gown to wear this winter except my black and my green one of Lierre,[41] and it is so cumbersome that I am tired of wearing it.

As for the girdle that my father promised me, I spoke to him about it a little before he last went to London, and he said to me it was your fault for not remembering to have it made. But I believe that is not so – he only said it as an excuse. I entreat you, if you venture to undertake it, that you will undertake to have it made before you come home. Because I have never had a greater need than I have now, because I have grown so elegant that I cannot fit into any of the waistbands or girdles that I have except one.

---

[39] As with 'my daughter' or 'my son', 'my mother' and 'my father' refer interchangeably to either biological relatives or relatives by marriage.

[40] See note 17.

[41] Another woollen cloth named after the Low Countries town, where it was produced.

Elizabeth Peverel[42] has been ill for 15 or 16 weeks with sciatica, but she has sent a message to my mother by Kate[43] that she should come here when God should grant the time, even if she must be wheeled in a barrow.

John of Damme was here, and your mother revealed my secret to him, and he said by his word of honour that nothing he had heard this year had pleased him more than this. I can no longer live by deception; I am found out by everyone who sees me. Everything else you wanted me to send you word of I have sent you word of in a letter that I wrote on Our Lady's Day just passed.

May the Holy Trinity protect you. Written at Oxnead in very great haste on the Thursday before St Thomas' Day.

I entreat you to wear the ring with the image of St Margaret that I sent you as a reminder until you come home.[44] You have left me such a reminder that makes me think about you both day and night when I would like to sleep. Yours, M.P.

No. 22: Margaret Paston to John Paston I.

In this letter, Margaret expresses concern for her husband who is recovering from an illness, again requests a new gown, and elliptically refers to her second pregnancy.

[28 September, probably 1443]

To my very honourable husband John Paston, living in the Inner Temple in London, in haste.

Most honourable husband, I commend myself to you, wishing with all my heart to hear of your welfare, thanking God for your improvement from the serious illness that you have had. And I thank you for the letter that you sent me, because on my word of honour, my mother and I have not been easy in our hearts from the time we knew of your illness until we knew for certain of your improvement. My mother promised another image of wax, of your weight, to Our Lady of Walsingham,[45] and she sent 4 nobles to the four orders of friars at Norwich to pray for you; and I have promised to go on pilgrimage to Walsingham and to St Leonard's[46] for

---

[42] Presumably the midwife.

[43] A family servant.

[44] St Margaret is the patron saint of childbirth and labour. I am grateful to Karen Cherewatuk for drawing my attention to this.

[45] The famous Norfolk shrine.

[46] A Norwich Priory.

you. On my word of honour, I have never had such a sorrowful time as I had from the time I knew of your illness until I knew of your improvement, and my heart is still not much at ease, nor shall be until I know that you are completely well.

Your father and mine was at Beccles a week ago today on business for the prior of Bromholm and he stayed at Geldeston that night and was there until 9 o'clock the next day. And I sent there for a gown and my mother said I would not be able to get any from there until I went back there; and accordingly they could not get one. My father[47] Garneys sent me word to say that he would be here next week, and my uncle as well, to amuse themselves here with their hawks; and they want to take me home with them. And so God help me I will excuse myself from going there if I can, because I believe I will sooner have news from you here than I would have there.

I shall send my mother a token that she gave to me, because I believe the time to send it to her has come, if I keep the promise I have made – I believe I have told you what it was. I entreat you with all my heart to undertake to send me a letter as quickly as possible, if writing is no trouble to you, and that you will undertake to send me word how your illness is. If I might have had my way I would have seen you before now. I would rather you were at home, if your comfort and illness could be as well looked after here as it is where you are now, than have a new gown, even if it were of scarlet.[48] I entreat you, if your illness is healed enough for you to bear to ride, when my father comes to London, to ask permission and come home when the horse is to be sent home again. Because I believe that you would be looked after as tenderly here as you are in London.

I do not have enough time to have written half a quarter as much as I would say to you if I could speak to you. I shall send you another letter as quickly as I can. Thank you if you undertake to remember my girdle and if you write to me now, because I imagine writing was not easy for you. May Almighty God protect you and send you health. Written at Oxnead in very great haste on St Michael's Eve.
Yours, M. PASTON.

My mother greets you well and sends you God's blessing and hers, and she entreats you, and I entreat you too, that you will eat and drink well, for that would be the greatest help to you now in respect of your health. Your son is doing well, blessed be God.

---

[47] Margaret's stepfather.
[48] A rich material.

No. 23: Margaret Paston to John Paston I.

The following year, Margaret writes to her husband from the residence of her mother and stepfather. She asks her husband for money and for properly-fitting caps for their sons, and passes on some local scandal.

[8 July 1444]

To my most honourable husband, John Paston.

Most respected and honourable husband, I commend myself to you, wishing with all my heart to hear of your health and happiness, thanking you for your letter, and for the things you sent with it. And with regard to John Eastgate, he has neither come here nor sent anything yet, so I believe I must borrow money in a little while unless you come home soon, because I believe I shall have none from him. God help me, I have only four shillings, and I owe nearly as much money as the aforementioned sum comes to.

I have carried out your errands to my mother and my uncle . . .

I entreat you to undertake to buy some lace for me matching the sample I send with this letter, and one piece of black lace. As for the caps that you sent me for the children, they are too small for them. I entreat you to buy them better and larger caps than those were. Also I entreat you to undertake to commend me to my father and mother, and tell her that all her children are in good health, blessed be God.

Heydon's[49] wife had a child on St Peter's Day. I heard it said that her husband will have nothing to do with her or with the last child that she had either. I heard it said that he said that if she came into his presence to make her excuses he would cut off her nose to let her be known for what she is, and if her child came into his presence he said he would kill it. He will not be persuaded by any means to take her back, so I heard say.

May the Holy Trinity protect you and send you health. Written at Geldeston on the first Wednesday after St Thomas' Day.

By yours, M. PASTON.

---

[49]   John Heydon was a lawyer and opponent of the Pastons. See also nos. 29, 37, 48 and 74. His son Harry is mentioned in nos. 67, 80 and 92. His grandson married the son of John III and Margery.

No. 24: Margaret Paston to John Paston I.

Margaret informs her husband of a conflict brewing over the Paston manor at Gresham. She reports that her own attempts at conciliating Lady Morley in a financial dispute had failed, but Agnes had made more progress. Margaret also tells her husband of a wedding.

[April 1448]

To my most honourable husband John Paston may this letter be delivered in haste.

Most honourable husband, I commend myself to you, wishing with all my heart to hear of your health and happiness, entreating you to know that I was with my Lady Morley on the Saturday after you left here, and told her the answer you had from John Butt. And she took it very coldly and said that she had told you and shown you enough for you to understand that the relief ought to be paid to her. And she said she knows very well that you are delaying it so that she will not have what belongs to her by right. And she told me how it was paid in Thomas Chaucer's[50] time, when her daughter Hastings was married. And she said that since you will not come to an agreement with her she will sue you for it, according to the law. I understood from her that she had been advised to proceed against you in this shortly. And then I entreated her to undertake not to proceed against you in this business until you come home. And she said no, by her faith, she would give you no more appointed time for this. She said she had given you so many appointed times to come to an agreement with her, only to have you break them, that she was really tired of it. And she said she was only a woman, she must do as her advisors say, and her advisors had advised her, and she said she would act accordingly. Then I entreated her again to wait until you come home. And I said I honestly believed that when you come home you would do what is fitting for you to do. And if you could be certain that it ought to be hers by legal right, I said I knew for certain that you would pay it very willingly, and told her that you had searched for documents relating to it, and you could find none at all. And she said she well knew that there were plenty of documents relating to it, and she has documents showing how Sir Robert of Mautby, and Sir John and my grandfather and various others of my ancestors paid it without ever objecting. And there was no way I could get her to undertake to leave off until you come home.

And she asked me to take a message to my mother, and when I got home I gave her the message. And she asked me if I had spoken to my lady about this aforementioned business, and I told her what I had done and the answer

---

[50] The son of the poet Geoffrey Chaucer.

I had been given. And she said she would go to my Lady Morley's the next day and she would speak to her about it, and try to get an agreement from her to leave off this business until you come home. And my mother certainly applied herself in this very faithfully, as my cousin Clere will tell you when he next speaks with you. And she has obtained an undertaking from my lady not to act against you in this matter, if you are willing to come to an agreement with her and to do as you ought between now and Trinity Sunday. . . .

Kathryn Walsam is to be married on the Monday following Trinity Sunday, so I am told, to the young gallant with the big chin. And a good array of gowns, girdles and garments, and many other fine clothes has been provided for her. And he has acquired a large income from land of five marks a year, to give her as her jointure.

I entreat you to undertake to send me word how you get on in the Gresham business, and whether Daniel is in favour. Harry Goneld has brought me 40 shillings from Gresham since you went, and he says I will have more at Whitsun if he can collect it. I believe James Gresham[51] has told you of other things that I have advanced since you went from here. If I hear of any hostile news in this region, I will send you word. I entreat you that I may be commended to my Lord Daniel.

May the Holy Trinity protect you and grant you good health, and prosperity in all business concerning your rights. Written at Norwich on the Wednesday after you left here.

Yours, MARGARET PASTON.

No. 25: Margaret Paston to John Paston I.

Margaret describes how John Wymondham, an associate of Lord Moleyns, who claimed ownership of the manor of Gresham, caused an affray on the street, insulting Margaret and her mother-in-law, attacking James Gloys, the family chaplain and threatening to kill him.

[19 May 1448]

Most honourable husband, I commend myself to you and entreat you to know that last Friday before noon, while the parson of Oxnead was at Mass in our parish church, exactly at the time of the elevation of the Host, James Gloys had been in the town, and came home past Wymondham's gate. And Wymondham stood in his gateway, and John Norwood, his man, stood next to him, and Thomas Hawes, his other man, stood in the street beside the gutter. And James Gloys passed between the men with his hat on his head,[52]

---

51   Gresham was an attorney who worked as an agent for William Paston I and John Paston I.

52   It is customary for men to remove their hats on meeting others as a sign of respect.

as he was accustomed to. And when Gloys was opposite Wymondham, he spoke thus, 'Cover thy head!' And Gloys replied 'So I will, for thee.'[53] And when Gloys had passed by the distance of 3 or 4 strides, Wymondham drew out his dagger and said 'Will thou do so, knave?' And with that Gloys turned round, and drew out his dagger and defended himself, fleeing into my mother's house. And Wymondham and his man Hawes threw stones and drove Gloys into my mother's house. And Hawes followed him into my mother's house, and threw a stone as big as a farthing loaf into the hall after Gloys, and then ran out of the house again. And Gloys followed him out and stood outside the gate, and then Wymondham called Gloys 'thief' and said he would die. And Gloys said he lied and called him 'churl', and told him to come himself or else the best man he had, and Gloys would answer him one on one. And then Hawes ran into Wymondham's house and fetched a spear and a sword, and gave his master his sword. And with the noise of this assault and attack my mother and I came out of the church from the consecration of the Host, and I told Gloys to go back into my mother's house, and he did so. And then Wymondham called my mother and me flagrant whores, and said the Pastons and all their family were . . .[54] Gimingham. We said he lied, knave and churl that he was. And he had plenty of offensive language, which you will know of later, by mouth.

After noon your mother and I went to the Prior of Norwich, and told him all about this incident, and the Prior sent for Wymondham, and meanwhile we went home again, and Pagrave came home with us. And while Wymondham was with the Prior, and we were at home in our houses, Gloys stood in the street at my mother's gate, and Hawes saw him there as he stood in Lady Hastings'[55] chamber. Immediately, he came down with a two-handed sword and assaulted the said Gloys again, and Thomas, my mother's man, and he let fly a stroke at Thomas with the sword and rippled his hand with it. And as for the latter assault, the parson of Oxnead saw it and will swear to it. And many other things were done, as Gloys can tell you, by mouth. And because of the danger which might come about because of the aforementioned matters and the circumstances to be avoided, on the advice of my mother and others, I am sending Gloys to serve you for a while to make my own heart easier. Because in good faith I would not for £40 have another disturbance like that. . . .

Lord Moleyn's servant is gathering up the rent at Gresham at a great pace, and James Gresham will tell you more openly about this when he arrives.

---

[53] The use of the informal forms 'thee' and 'thou' rather than the formal 'you' is extremely offensive.

[54] Hole in manuscript.

[55] Wymondham's wife.

No more at this time, but may Almighty God protect you. Written in haste on Trinity Sunday in the evening.

Yours, MARGARET PASTON.

. . . .When Wymondham said that James would die, I said to him that I believed he would regret it if he slew him or caused him any bodily harm. And he said no, he would never regret it nor come to a farthing's worth of harm even if he killed both you and him. And I said yes, if he killed the smallest child from your kitchen, if he did, he would be likely, I think, to die for it. I am told that he will go to London in haste. I entreat you to be careful how you go if he is there, because he is very vicious and malicious. I know well he will not attack you heroically, but I believe he will set upon you or on some of your men, like a thief. I entreat you with all my heart not to let James come home again at all until you come home, to put my heart at ease, because upon my word of honour I would not have him or any of your men hurt in your absence, for £20. And indeed he is very hated both by Wymondham and certain of his men, and by others to whom Wymondham tells his tale as he pleases, because wherever Wymondham tells his tale he makes them believe that James is guilty and that he is not guilty at all.

I entreat you with all my heart to hear mass and the other services you are obliged to, with a devout heart, and I truly hope that you will prosper well in all your business by the grace of God. Trust truly in God and love him and serve him, and he will not deceive you. I will send you word of any other business in haste.

No. 26: Margaret Paston to John Paston I.[56]

Margaret, who has taken up residence in a manor house in Gresham, and who fears an attack by Lord Moleyns and his men, writes to her husband requesting weapons and armour, and notifies him of the reports of their spies. She also asks him to purchase cloth for clothes and other domestic items.

[1448]

Most honourable husband, I commend myself to you, and entreat you to get some crossbows and windlasses[57] to bend them with, and bolts, because your houses here are so low that no one can shoot out with longbows, even if we might have ever so much need. I believe you could get such things from Sir John Fastolf, if you sent to him. And also I would like you to get two or three short poleaxes to defend the doors with, and as many jacks[58] as you can.

---

[56] This letter has no address or signature.
[57] Instruments for bending crossbows.
[58] Defensive leather coats.

Partridge and his company of men are very afraid that you will take possession again by force, and they have made great preparations inside the house, so I am told. They have made bars to bar across the doors, and they have made loopholes in every quarter of the house to shoot out of, both with bows and with handguns. And those holes that have been made for hand-guns are scarcely knee-high from the floor, and five such holes have been made. No man could shoot out of them with hand-bows.

Purry found himself in the company of William Hasard at Querles', and told him that he would come and drink with Partridge and with him. And he said he would be welcome; and after noon he went there to observe what they did and what company they had with them. And when he arrived there the doors were fastened securely and there was nobody inside except Marriott and Capron and his wife and Querles' wife and another man in black who limped a little; I believe from what he said that it was Norfolk of Gimingham. And the said Purry observed all these aforementioned things, and Marriott and his company spoke many angry words, which you will be told of when you come home.

I entreat you that you will undertake to have 1lb of almonds and 1lb of sugar bought for me, and that you will have some frieze[59] bought to make your children's gowns. You will get the cheapest and the most choice from Hay's wife, so I am told. And, if you could, buy a yard of black broadcloth for a hood for me, at 44d or 4s a yard, for there is neither good cloth nor good frieze in this town. As for the children's gowns, if I have cloth I shall get them made. May the Trinity protect you and send you good fortune in all your business.

No. 27: Margaret Paston to John Paston I.

Having been forcefully evicted from the manor in Gresham at the end of January 1449, Margaret took refuge with the wife of one of the Paston's supporters, John of Damme in their residence at Sustead. Margaret writes to her husband, telling him that she sent a servant with a message to Lord Moleyns' men, and of her subsequent confrontation with them. She warns her husband of the dangers in London.

[15 February 1449]

To my most honourable master John Paston may this be delivered in haste.

Most honourable husband, I commend myself to you, wishing with all my heart to hear how you are. . . .

---

[59] A course woollen cloth.

I sent Katherine to take the aforementioned message, because I could get no man to take it, and sent James Halman and Henry Holt with her. And she asked Barow for an answer to her message, and whether the aforementioned men would be able to live in peace, and otherwise some redress would have to made to them. And he gave her, and those that were with her, a warm welcome, and said that he wanted to talk to me, if it would not displease me. And Katherine told him that she believed that I did not wish to speak with him. And he said he would come past this house while hunting after noon, and no one would come with him except Hegon and one of his own men, and he would then bring an answer that would please me. And after noon they came here and sent a message in to me to find out whether they could speak with me, and entreated to speak with me. And they waited outside the gates all the time, and I came out to them and spoke with them outside, and begged to be excused for not bringing them into the house. I said that because they felt no good will towards the master of the house I would not take it upon myself to admit them to the mistress. They said I did right. And then we walked on and I asked them for an answer to the message I had sent to them. They said to me they had brought an answer that they thought would please me, and told me how they had conferred with their companions about the business I had asked them about, and that they could undertake that none of the men mentioned, nor any of your men, would be injured either because of them nor any of their companions. And they assured me about that on their words of honour. Nevertheless, I do not trust their promises, since I find them dishonest in other things.

I clearly understood from them that they regretted what they had done. Barow swore to me on his word that he would rather his lord had not commanded him to come to Gresham than have 40 shillings and another 40. And he said he was very sorry about this because he had known you before; he was very sorry about what was done. I said that he ought to have compassion for you and others who had been wrongfully dispossessed of their property, because he had been dispossessed himself. And he said he did, and told me that he had applied to my lord of Suffolk sundry times, and would go on doing until he got his property again. I told him that you had applied to my Lord Moleyns sundry times for the manor of Gresham since you were dispossessed, and could never get a reasonable answer from him, and therefore you took possession again, believing that it was for the best. And he said he would never blame my lord of Suffolk for taking possession of his property, because he said that my said lord was encouraged in it by the advice of a dishonest villain. And I told him that the same applies to the business between Lord Moleyns and you.

I told him I knew very well that he did not undertake it from any rightful claim to the manor of Gresham, but only by the advice of a dishonest villain. I repeated no name but it seemed to me that they knew whom I meant. We said much more, which would take a long time to write down. I repeated to them that it was said that I would not be living so near them for much longer, and they denied it was ever said, as they do various other things, that never said they were, and many things that I know for certain were said.

I hear it said that you and John of Damme are constantly under threat, and it is said that even though you are in London you will be met with there just as if you were here. And therefore I entreat you with all my heart to be careful how you go there and to take good companions with you when you go out. Lord Moleyns has a company of ruffians with him who do not care what they do, and they are the sort who are to be feared most. Those that are at Gresham say that they have not done as much harm to you as they were commanded to do. . . .

I entreat you with all my heart to send me word how you are and how you get on in your business, because I swear on my word of honour that I cannot be entirely easy in my heart, nor shall be, until I hear news of how you are.

Most of your possessions that were at Gresham have been sold and given away. Barow and his companion spoke to me in a most pleasant manner, and it seems to me that they would gladly please me. They said they would serve me and please me if it lay in their power to do anything for me, except for things that belonged to their lord by right. I told them that as for the sort of services they had done to you and me, I would not want them to do any more, either to you or to me. They said I could have had whatever I wanted from them from Gresham, and as much as I had wanted. I said no, if I could have had what I wanted I would have left neither the house nor the possessions that were in it. They said as for the possessions, they were insignificant. I said you would not have given away the possessions that were in the house when they went in, not for £100. They said the possessions they saw there were scarcely worth £20.

As for your mother and mine, she is well, blessed be God, and she has still had nothing but good news, blessed be God.

May the Blessed Trinity protect you and grant you health and good fortune in all your business. Written at Sustead on the first Saturday after Saint Valentine's Day. Here in this region no one dares to say a good word about you, may God put it right.

Yours, M.P.

No. 28: Margaret Paston to John Paston I.[60]

Following warnings of a plot to kidnap her, Margaret flees Sustead and takes refuge in Norwich. She writes to her husband to explain her actions. She also warns him that his enemies may attempt to poison him. Margaret provides livery for Purry, who previously acted as her spy.

[28 February 1449]

Most honourable husband, I commend myself to you, wishing with all my heart to hear of your health and happiness, entreating you not to be displeased because I have left the house which you left me in. Because on my word of honour, such tidings were brought to me by various people who wished you and me well – I shall let you know who when you come home – that I dared not stay there any longer. It was made known to me that several of Lord Moleyns' men said that if they could get me they wanted to abduct me and imprison me inside the castle, and then they said they wanted you to come and get me out. And they said it would only make you a little angry. And after I heard these tidings, my heart was not at ease until I got here. And I dared not go out of the house I was in until I was ready to set off. Nor did anyone in the house know I was coming here except the mistress, not an hour before I came here. And I told her I was coming here to have the clothes I wanted made for me and the children, and said that I believed I would be here a fortnight or three weeks. I entreat you to keep secret the reason for my departure until I speak with you, for those who warned me about this do not on any account want it revealed.

I spoke with your mother on my way, and she offered, if you want, that I should stay in this town. She was very eager that we should stay in her house, and has given me what goods she could spare to keep house with until you are supplied with a place and goods of your own to keep house with. I entreat you to send me word by the bearer of this, how you want me to act. I would be very sorry to live as close to Gresham as I did, until this business between Lord Moleyns and you is fully resolved.

Barow told me that there were no better title deeds in England than Lord Moleyns has for the manor of Gresham. I told him I believed that they were the same sort of deeds that Willam Hasard said yours were: he said the seals on them were not yet cold. I said I believed his lord's deeds were like that. I said I knew for certain about your deeds, no one could have any better than you have, and I said that the seals on them were two hundred years older than he is. The said Barow said to me that if he went to London while you were there he would drink with you, to dispel any ill-feeling between

---

you. He said he acted merely as a servant; and did what he was commanded to. Purry will tell you what conversation took place between Barow and me when I came back from Walsingham. I entreat you with all my heart for God's sake to beware of Lord Moleyns and his men. Though they may speak ever so pleasantly to you, do not trust them, nor eat nor drink with them, because they are so dishonest they cannot be trusted. And also I entreat you to be careful what you eat or drink in any other company, for people are so untrustworthy.

I entreat you with all my heart to undertake to send me word by the bearer of this, of how you are and how you are getting on with your business. I am very surprised that you have not sent me more tidings than you have sent. . . .

I have given Purry a gown. I entreat you to take note of it and send me word if you want me to arrange for all your liveries to be the same. The price of a yard of it is 13d ob[61] so I think it is well worth it. . . .

May the Holy Trinity protect you. Written in Norwich on the first Friday after Ash Wednesday.

No. 29: Margaret Paston to John Paston I.

Margaret writes to her husband to tell him that Lord Moleyns stands by his claim to Gresham, and to report on the activity of John Hauteyn, a Carmelite friar who, some years before, had asserted his right to Oxnead, Agnes' jointure. Shortly after the death of Edmond Paston I in late March, Margaret requests that his books be sent to his brother William Paston II, a student in Cambridge.

[2 April 1449]

To my most honourable master John Paston, living in the Inner Temple, may this be delivered in haste.

Most honourable husband, I commend myself to you, wishing you to know that my cousin Clere dined with me today, and she told me that Heydon had been with her late yesterday evening. And he told her that he had a letter from Lord Moleyns, and showed her that letter, entreating him to tell his friends and well-wishers in this area that he thanks them for their good will and for what they have done for him, and also entreating him to tell Richard Arnold of Cromer that he was sorry and ill pleased that his men had attacked him. Because he said it was not his wish that his men should attack anyone in the area without very good reason. And as for what was done to you, if it could be proved that he had acted illegally regarding your

---

[61] See note 20 above.

moveable goods, you could rest assured that you would have reason to thank him. And he entreated Heydon in the letter to report in the area that he would do this if he had not acted as he ought.

The friar that claimed Oxnead was in this town yesterday and today, and was lodged at Berry's, and this afternoon he set off, but I do not know to where. He said openly in this town that he will have Oxnead, and that he has the support of Lord Suffolk, who will be his patron in this matter. Someone warned your mother in the last couple of days that she ought to be careful, because they said openly that she was likely to be served as you were served at Gresham, within a very short time. Also Lord Moleyns wrote in the aforementioned letter that he would, with his body and his goods, staunchly stand by all those who had been his friends and supporters in the Gresham business. And he entreated Heydon to give them a message that they should not be at all afraid, because what was done would be adhered to.

My mother entreats you to send my brother William at Cambridge a *nominale* and a book of sophistry which were my brother Edmond's, which my same brother promised my mother the last time he spoke to her that he would have sent to my brother William.

May the blessed Trinity protect you. Written at Norwich in haste on the Wednesday before Palm Sunday.

Yours, M.P.

No. 30: Margaret Paston to John Paston I.

Margaret writes to her husband and reports that he has the support of Lady Felbrigg in the Gresham conflict. She also provides news of family and friends.

[1 July 1451]

To my honourable husband John Paston may this be delivered in haste.

Most honourable husband, I commend myself to you, wishing with all my heart to hear of your health and happiness, entreating you to know that I have spoken to Lady Felbrigg about what you asked me to talk to her about. And she said openly that she would not and never intended either to let Lord Moleyns or any other have their way in that business for as long as she lives. . . . I had dinner at Topps' on St Peter's Day. Lady Felbrigg and the other ladies there wished you had been there. They said they would all have been the merrier if you had been there. My cousin Topps is very anxious until she may hear good tidings about her brother's business. She said that there should be an appointment this coming Monday between her brother and Sir Andrew Ogard and Wymondham. I entreat you to let me know how they get on, and how you progress in your own business too.

Also, I entreat you with all my heart to send me a pot of medicine in haste, because both I and your daughter have suffered greatly since you left here. And one of the most handsome young men of this parish is very ill with the pestilence; God knows how he will get on. I have sent my uncle Berney the pot of medicine you had bought for him. My aunt commends herself to you and entreats you to do on her behalf that which is mentioned in the letter that I send with this letter, and whatever you consider best to do in this matter.

Sir Harry Inglose passed to God last night, may God absolve his soul, and was carried to St Faith's at 9 o'clock today, and will be buried there. If you want to buy any of his possessions I entreat you to send word to me in haste, and I will speak to Robert Inglose and Witchingham about it. I believe they are the executors.

May the blessed Trinity protect you. Written at Norwich in a hurry on the first Thursday after St Peter's Day.

Yours, M.P.

I entreat you, do not trust the sheriff, for all his fine words.

No. 31: Margaret Paston to John Paston I.

Margaret passes on a message to her husband from his sister Elizabeth concerning her ongoing marriage negotiations, and informs him about Agnes' misgivings. She also asks for a necklace and a new girdle.

[30 January, perhaps 1453]

To my most honourable husband John Paston may this be delivered in haste.

Most honourable husband, I commend myself to you, entreating you to know that I spoke to my sister yesterday, and she told me she was sorry not to have spoken with you before you went. And she requests, if it pleases you, that you speak with the gentleman of whom you know, in such a way that he might understand that you would be well disposed towards the matter that you know about. Because she told me that he has previously said that he understood that you did not value it much. Therefore she entreats you to be her good brother, and to get a final answer now as to whether it will be yes or no. Because her mother has said to her since you left that she is not well disposed towards it, it will prove deceptive, and she says to her there is a great skill in whitewashing. And she speaks to her in a way that she thinks is very unfriendly, and she is very tired of it. Therefore, she would rather have it finally concluded. She says that all her trust is in you, and whatever you do about it she will agree to it.

Master Brackley was here yesterday to speak with you. I spoke with him, but he would not tell me what his errand was. It is said around here that the sessions shall be at Thetford on this coming Saturday, and my lord of Norfolk and others will be there, with important people, so it is said. We have no other tidings as yet.

May the Blessed Trinity protect you. Written at Norwich on the Tuesday before Candlemas. I beg you that you will undertake to remember to buy something for my neck, and to get my girdle made.

Yours, M.P.

My cousin Crane commends herself to you and begs you to remember her business, etc., because she cannot sleep at nights because of him.

No. 32: Margaret Paston to John Paston I.

Margaret tells her husband about a royal visit to Norwich, and complains about her lack of appropriate jewellery.

[20 April 1453]

To my very honourable master John Paston may this be delivered in haste.

Most honourable husband, I commend myself to you, entreating you to know that the man from Knapton who owes you money sent me 39s 8d this week, and, as for the remainder of the money, he has promised to bring it at Whitsun. And as for the priest, Howard's son, he went to Cambridge last week, and will not come home again until midsummer, and so I cannot do your errand.

As for news, the Queen[62] came to this town last Tuesday afternoon and stayed here until 3 o'clock on Thursday afternoon, and she sent Shernborne to ask my cousin, Elizabeth Clere, to come to her. And she did not dare to disobey her command, and went to her. And when she came into the Queen's presence, the Queen made much of her, and encouraged her to find a husband, which you will know about in due course. But as for that, he is no nearer than he was before. The Queen was very pleased with her answer, and spoke of her very approvingly, and said on her word of honour that since she came to Norfolk she had seen no gentlewoman who pleases her more than she does.

Blake, the bailiff of Swaffham, was here with the King's brother. And he came to me assuming that you were at home, and said that the King's brother asked him to entreat you, in his name, to come to him, because he would have been very pleased if you had come to him if you had been at home. And he told me he was certain you should be sent for when he came to

---

[62] Margaret of Anjou, wife of Henry VI.

London, because of both Costessey and other things. I entreat you to spend some money on me before Whitsun, so that I can have something for my neck. When the Queen was here I borrowed my cousin Elizabeth Clere's ornament, because I dare not, out of shame, in my beads go in the midst of so many lovely gentlewomen who were here at that time.

May the blessed Trinity protect you. Written in Norwich on the Friday before St George's Day.

By yours, M. PASTON.

No. 33: Margaret Paston to John Paston I.

Margaret apologizes to her husband for angering him, and tells him about various errands she has undertaken.

[15 October, perhaps 1453]

To my very honourable husband John Paston may this be delivered in haste.

Most honourable husband, I commend me to you, entreating that you should not be displeased with me even though my foolishness made you displeased with me. Upon my word of honour, I do not wish to do or say anything that should make you displeased with me, and if I have done, I am sorry for it, and will make up for it. Therefore I entreat you to forgive me and not to be ill disposed in your heart towards me, because your displeasure should be too grievous for me to endure.

I send you the roll that you sent for, sealed within, by the bearer of this; it was found in your trunk. And as for herring, I have bought a horse load for 4s 6d; I cannot get any more yet. As for drink, I have been promised some, but I cannot get it yet.

I sent a message to Joan Petche to get an answer about the windows, because she cannot come to me, and she sent me word that she had spoken to Thomas Ingham. And he said that he ought to speak with you himself and he would come to an agreement with you easily enough, and said to her that it was not up to her to ask him to block the lights.[63] And also it was not up to him to do it because the house is his only for a few years. And as for all the other errands that you have ordered me to do, they will be done as soon as possible.

May the Blessed Trinity protect you. Written in Norwich on the Monday after St Edward's Day.

Yours, M.P.

---

[63] Verticle sections between the mullions of a window.

No. 34: Margaret Paston to John Paston I.

Margaret informs her husband of the progress of the building of a new residence in Norwich, and tells him about Agnes' growing desperation to see Elizabeth married.

[29 January, perhaps 1454]

To my very honourable husband John Paston may this be delivered in haste.

Most honourable husband, I commend myself to you, wishing to hear of your health and happiness, entreating you to know that Sir Thomas Howes[64] has provided four beams for the private room and the malthouse and the brewery, of which he has bought three. And the fourth, which will be the longest and biggest of all, he will get from Hellesdon, which he says my master Fastolf will give me because my chamber will be made with it. As for laying the said beams, they will be laid next week because of the malthouse, and as for the rest, I believe it will wait till you come home because I can obtain neither joists nor planks yet. I have measured the private room where you would like your chests and your counting table to be placed for now. And there is no space beside the bed, even if the bed were to be moved to the door, in order to place both your table and your chests there and to have space to go and sit next to it. Therefore I have arranged that you will have the same private room that you had previously, where you will sleep. And when your belongings are moved out of your little house the door will be locked and your bags placed in one of the large chests so that they will be safe, I trust. . . .

My mother entreats you to remember my sister, and to play your part faithfully in helping to get her a good marriage before you come home. It seems from my mother's words that she would never be so glad to be free of her as she is now. She has been told that Knyvett the heir is to marry. Both his wife and children are dead, so she was told, so she would like you to enquire whether it is so or not, and what property he has, and whether you think he should be spoken to about it. I entreat you not to be reluctant to write letters to me between now and when you come home. If I could I would have one from you every day.

May the Blessed Trinity protect you. Written at Norwich on the Tuesday after the Conversion of St Paul.

By yours, M.P.

---

[64] Howes was servant and chaplain to Sir John Fastolf. He initially supported Paston claims to Fastolf's estates, but subsequently changed sides in the dispute.

No. 35: Margaret Paston to John Paston I.[65]

Margaret reports on John Wymondham's decision to sell the rights to profit from any future marriage negotiations for his son in order to finance his plans for his second marriage to the mother of one of Margaret's relatives.

[September, about 1459]

Most honourable husband, I commend myself to you. . . .

Wymondham's errand to Lady Suffolk was to request her patronage, and to beg her to speak to my cousin Heveningham about having his support, because he lives in hope of marrying his mother. And he has made attempts to get her, with the help of John Gros and his wife, and Bokenham and various others, and offers to find surety to clear her husband's debts, which come to 300 marks, and to pay them off in one day. And to this end, so he says, he has made a bargain with a London merchant, and sold him the right to arrange his son's marriage, for which he will get 700 marks, of which 300 marks will go towards the aforesaid debt. And also he offers to give her the manor of Felbrigg as her jointure, and makes other generous offers, as you will hear later. As for the support of my cousin Heveningham, he says Wymondham will never have it, not in order to get her property. He [Heveningham] feels sad in his soul about it, because he is afraid that if the generous offers are realised she will have him. My same cousin begs you, out of respect for God, to do your best to stop this if you can. He will be here again on St Michael's Eve. He was really sorry that you were out this time, because he believed that you could have done a lot of good at this time. He has said as much against it as he can do and still retain his mother's good will. Lady Suffolk sent one letter to her yesterday by Stanley, who is known as a man very dear to my said lady, requesting her in her letter to show support and favour to Wymondham in what he wanted from her, and about other matters that you shall hear about later. Because I expect she will show you that same letter, and take you into her confidence in many things. And I shall play my part in hindering Wymondham's plans as best I can until you come home. I beg you to send me a copy of his pedigree, so that I can show her how honourable it is. Because she has been informed, in good faith, by her noble son Gros, and by Bokenham, that he is more honourable in birth and property than they or any others can prove, so I believe. I beg you not to let this matter be made public until you hear more about it, or afterwards, for my cousin Heveningham told me much

---

[65] This letter has no address or signature.

of it in secret, and other things which you will know of when you come home, etc.

In haste, in all haste.

No. 36: Margaret Paston to John Paston I.

Writing shortly after the death of Sir John Fastolf, Margaret tells her husband that she has been making enquiries about the appropriate manner of celebrating Christmas in a bereaved household. Caister Castle was the manor belonging to Fastolf, to which John Paston laid claim.

[24 December, probably 1459]

Most honourable husband, I commend myself to you. May it please you to know that I sent your eldest son to Lady Morley to find out what games were played in her house on the Christmas following the death of her husband. And she said there was no masquerading, nor harp nor lute playing, nor singing, nor any loud pastime, only backgammon and chess and cards. She gave her people permission to play these games and no other. Your son did his errand very well, as you shall hear subsequently. I sent your younger son to Lady Stapleton, and she agreed with what Lady Morley said, in accordance with what she had seen practised in honourable houses where she has been.

I entreat you to try to get someone at Caister to look after your buttery because the man you left with me will not take it upon himself to make up the accounts daily as you commanded. He says he has not been used to calculating expenditure on either bread or beer until the end of the week, and he says he knows well that he would not be able to do it. And therefore I believe he cannot stay. And I believe you will be obliged to provide another man in exchange for Simond, because you are never the nearer a wise man with him.

I am sorry that you will not be at home for Christmas. I entreat you to come as soon as you can. I shall consider myself half a widow because you are not at home, etc. May God protect you. Written on Christmas Eve.

By your, M.P.

No. 37: Margaret Paston to John Paston I.

In the turbulent fortnight between Margaret of Anjou's victory at the second battle of St Albans on 17 February 1461 and the enthronement of Edward IV on 4 March, Margaret warns her husband of a plot to hand him over to his enemies.

[1 March, probably 1461]

May it please you to know that it has been made known to me by someone who is well disposed towards you that, if you come here freely, an ambush has been set in this district. They plan to conduct you into the presence of such a lord in the North who will not help you, but will be a danger to your life or great and insupportable loss of your property. And he who has now taken this enterprise upon himself was under-sheriff to G. Saintlow. He has great support in this due to the influence of the son of William Baxter who lies buried in Grey Friars.[66] And it is reported that this son has given much silver to the lords in the North to accomplish the business. And now he and all his old companions are getting busy and are very ready for action and merry, confident that everything is and will be as he would like it. I am also told that the father of the Bastard[67] in this district said that this county should now be secured for him and his heirs also; by which I understand they think they have no enemy except you etc. Therefore please be more careful in managing the safety of your person, and also do not be too hasty to come into this district until you hear that the world is safer. I believe the bearer of this will tell you more by mouth of what he will be informed about the disturbance in this district.

May God protect you. Written in haste on the second Sunday in Lent by candlelight in the evening.

By yours, etc. M.

No. 38: Margaret Paston to John Paston I.

In this letter, Margaret expresses her relief to hear that her husband has been released from the Fleet Prison, where he had been imprisoned for a short time (this was one of a series of periods of imprisonment). She tells him of the support he has in the locality.

[2 November 1461]

Most honourable husband, I commend myself to you. May it please you to know that I received your letter that you sent me by John Holme last Wednesday. And I also received another letter on Friday night, that you sent me by Nicholas Newman's man, for which letters I thank you, because I should otherwise have thought it had been worse for you than it has been, or will be, by the grace of Almighty God. And yet I could not be happy after I had the last letter until today when the mayor sent me a message and sent me word that he had reliable knowledge that you were released from the Fleet and that Howard was committed there after various serious complaints were made to the King about him. It was said in Norwich and in several other

---

[66] John Heydon (see note 49 above). Heydon was of obscure birth and had changed his name from Baxter.

[67] Sir Thomas Tuddenham (executed in 1462).

places in the district last Saturday that you were committed to the Fleet, and in good faith, as I heard say, people were very sorry about it, both in Norwich and in the district. You and all those who love you are greatly obliged to thank God that you are as greatly loved by people as you are. You are under great obligation to the mayor, and to Gilbert, and to several other aldermen, because they loyally support you, as much as it is in their power to do so.

I have spoken with Sir Thomas Howes about the things you wrote to me about. And he promised me he would try to carry out your purpose as fast as he could. And in good faith, as my brother and Playter can tell you, from what he said to us he is and will be loyal to you. And as for William Worcester,[68] he has been made to feel so anxious, by the parson and others, as my brother and Playter will tell you, that they hope he will do well enough. The parson spoke very well and plainly to him. The parson told him that he had spoken to Sir William Chamberlain and his wife, and he thinks they will do well enough according to your purpose if they are entreated politely. The parson told me he knew for certain that Sir William Chamberlain could be of more assistance in these matters you wrote about regarding my lord of Bedford than any man alive today. Also he told me that he understood from them that they would support you strongly if you would support them. The parson truly believes he can bring you to an agreement when he comes to London.

Also, my brother and Playter were with Calthorp to ask about the matter you wrote to me about. They will tell you the answer he gave them. I sent the parson of Hellesdon to Gurney to speak to him about the same matter, and he said in good faith no such thing was asked of him, and if it had been asked he would neither have said nor done anything against you. He said he had always found you loving and faithful to him, and so he said he would be the same to you if it was in his power, entreating me not to think otherwise. As for John Gros, he is at Sloley, therefore he could not be spoken with.

I entreat you to send me word whether you want me to leave here, because it is beginning to grow cold staying here. Sir Thomas Howes and John Russe will resolve everything according to your purpose as much as they are able to this week, and he intends to come afterwards to you on the Monday after St Leonard's Day. My brother and Playter would have been with you before now, but they wanted to remain here until today was over because of the shire court. I spoke with my brother William as you asked me to. And he told me, so God help him, that he hired two horses two days before you went, in order to go with you, and because you did not ask him to go with you, he said that he believed you did not want him with you.

---

[68] Worcester was another important Fastolf servant. He opposed John Paston I's claims to the estates.

Thomas Fastolf's mother was here on the day after you went to speak to you on her son's behalf. She entreats you, out of respect to God, that you will support him, and help him to assert his rights and get his property out of the hands of those that have had it in his minority. She said that they want to make him out to be a year younger than he is, but she says that he is over 21, and she would dare to take an oath on that.

And may the Blessed Trinity protect you, and grant you good fortune in all your business, and grant victory over all your enemies. Written in haste on All Souls' Day.

By yours, M.P.

No. 39: Margaret Paston to John Paston I.

Margaret expresses her concern that she has not heard from her husband for some time, and updates him about the attempts being made to restore order in the area, in which rebellion is brewing.

[7 January 1462]

To my most honourable husband John Paston may this be delivered in haste.

Most honourable husband, I commend myself to you. May it please you to know that I sent you a letter by Berney of Witchingham's man, which was written on St Thomas' Day during Christmas, and I have had no news or letter from you since the week before Christmas, which I am greatly surprised about. I am afraid that all is not well with you because you did not come home or send a message before now. I truly believed you would have been home by Twelfth Night at the latest. I entreat you with all my heart to undertake to send me word of how you are as hastily as you can, because my heart will never be at ease until I have news of you.

People around here begin to grow rowdy, and it is said here that my Lord Clarence and the Duke of Suffolk are coming down with certain other judges to try such people who are rumoured to be riotous in this district. And also it is said here that a new rescue has been submitted in response to that which was done at the last shire court. I believe such talk comes from the dishonest villains who want to spread rumours around the district. People here say they would rather all go up together to the King and complain of such dishonest villains as they have been wronged by in the past than be complained about without reason and be hanged at their own doors. In good faith, people here have a very great fear of a rising amongst the common people, unless a better solution can be found in haste to appease the people, and someone impartial to whom the people are well disposed is sent down to impose order. They have no love at all for the Duke of Suffolk or his mother.[69] They say that all the traitors and extortionists of this district are maintained by them, and by those they can bribe, with the intention of maintaining still the extortion that was carried out by those who were in authority before. People believe that if the Duke of Suffolk comes there will be a malicious regime unless others come who are better loved here than he is.

People have a greater fear of injury because you and my cousin Berney do not come home. They say they know for certain that it is not well with you, and if it is not well with you they say they are sure that those who want to wrong you will soon wrong them, and that makes them almost mad. May God in his holy mercy grant grace that there may be a good and sensible regime established in this area in haste, because I never heard of so much robbery and manslaughter around here in such a short time as there is now.

And as for gathering rent, I never knew a worse period, because Richard Calle[70] says he can get only a little money of what is owed, either from your estate or Fastolf's. And John Paston says that those best able to pay, pay least. They act as if they were expecting a new world.

And may the Blessed Trinity protect you and send us good news of you. Yelverton[71] is a very poor friend to you and to others in this area, so I am told. Written in a hurry on the first Thursday after Twelfth Night.
By your, MARGARET PASTON.

No. 40: Margaret Paston to John Paston I.

Margaret writes to her husband that in the opinion of Agnes, given the unstable political and thus financial climate, a husband should be sought for their daughter Margery.

[13 November, probably 1463]

To my most honourable husband John Paston may this letter be delivered in haste.

Most honourable husband, I commend myself to you. May it please you to know that I was in Norwich this week to buy such things as I need in preparation for winter. And I was at my mother's, and while I was there a man, one Wroth, a kinsman of Elizabeth Clere, came in, and he saw your daughter and praised her to my mother, and said that she was a fine young woman. And my mother entreated him to find her a good marriage, if he

---

[69] The Duke of Suffolk's mother was Alice, granddaughter of Geoffrey Chaucer.
[70] Calle was manager of the Pastons' estates. He married Margaret's daughter, Margery (see no. 60), causing a rift within the family, but remained in their service.
[71] Sir William Yelverton was a lawyer and advisor to Fastolf who sided against the Pastons in the dispute over Fastolf's will.

knew of any. And he said he knew someone who was worth 100 marks a year, who is the son of Sir John Cley who is chamberlain of my lady of York; and he is 18 years old. If you think it is to be spoken of my mother believes that, with the world the way it is, it could be arranged for less money than it should be in future, either that or some other good marriage.

Also, I spoke to Master John Eastgate about Pickering's business in accordance with your purpose in the letter that you sent home. And he said to me that he would write to you about how he had acted in it, and so he sent you a letter which was sent to you by John Woodhouse's man with other letters. As for an answer to the other business, Daubeney[72] tells me he wrote to you.

I entreat Almighty God to protect you. Written at Caister the first Sunday after St Martin's Day.

By your M. PASTON.

No. 41: Margaret Paston to John Paston II.

In this, the first surviving letter from Margaret to her eldest son, written shortly after he had been knighted, she reproves him for angering his father and causing a rift between herself and her husband. Margaret is also concerned about the marriage prospects of one of the servants.

[15 November 1463]

To my dearly beloved son Sir John Paston may this be delivered in haste.

I greet you warmly, and send you God's blessing and mine, letting you know that I have received a letter from you which you delivered to Master Roger at Lynn, from which I understand that you think you did not conduct yourself well in leaving here without my knowledge. Therefore I am letting you know I was very displeased with you. Your father thought, and still thinks, that I had agreed to your leaving, and that has made me very sad. I believe he will be a good father to you from now on if you conduct yourself well and do as you ought towards him. And I order you, upon my blessing, that in anything concerning your father that should be to his honour, profit or benefit to apply yourself and to do your best with all diligence to further it, if you want to have my good wishes. And that will make your father be a better father to you. I was told that you sent him a letter to London. What was the purpose of it I do not know. But even though he took it lightly, I would like you not to spare from writing to him again as humbly as you can, begging him to be your good father. And send him whatever tidings

---

[72] Like Calle, John Daubeney was in the employ of the Paston family. He died at their service in the siege of Caister.

there are from the district you are in, and be more careful in your expenditure than you have been before now, and look after your own money. I believe that you will find it the most profitable to you. I would like you to send me word how you get on, and how you have raised money for yourself since you left here, by some trustworthy man, without your father knowing about it. I dare not let him know about the last letter you wrote to me, because he was very displeased with me at that time.

Also, I want you to speak with Wykes and find out how he is disposed towards Jane Walsham. She has said, since he left here, that unless she can have him she will never be married; her heart is very set on him. She told me that he told her there was no woman in the world he loved so much. I would not want him to deceive her, because she speaks in good faith, and if he will not have her, let me know hastily, and I shall arrange something else for her.

As for your harness and gear that you left here, it is in Daubeney's keeping. It has not been moved since you left because he did not have the keys. I believe it will deteriorate unless it is attended to soon. Your father does not know where it is. I sent your grey horse to Ruston to the farrier, and he says he shall never be any good for riding nor much good for ploughing nor pulling a cart. And he says he was splayed and his shoulder torn from the body. I do not know what to do with him. Your grandmother would be glad to hear some tidings from you. It would be well done if you were to send a letter to her saying how you are getting on as hastily as you can.

And may God protect you and make a good man of you, and give you grace to do as well as I would like you to. Written at Caister the Tuesday before the Feast of St Edmund the King.

Your mother, M. PASTON.

I would like you to make much of the parson of Filby, the bearer of this, and to give him a warm welcome if you can.

No. 42: Margaret Paston to John Paston I.

The Paston property disputes continued to escalate, and John de la Pole, 2nd Duke of Suffolk, laid claim to the manors of Hellesdon and Drayton. (On the conflict over Hellesdon, see nos. 42–46, 48–55, 58, 67 and 76.) John II had not yet been allowed to resume his role in his father's household. Margaret writes to her husband entreating him to forgive his son and receive him with kindness.

[8 April 1465]

To my honourable husband John Paston may this be delivered in haste.

Most honourable husband, I commend myself to you. May it please you to know that I am sending you a copy of a deed that John Edmonds of

Taverham sent to me by means of Dorlet. He told Dorlet that he had such a deed as he believed would assist in verifying the right of ownership that is claimed by the Duke of Suffolk in Drayton. Because on the same deed he sent me the seal of his coat of arms is like the copy I am sending you, and nothing like that of the Duke of Suffolk's ancestors. Also, the said Edmonds says that if he can find anything else that could assist you in that business he will play his part in it. Also, John Russe sent me word that Barker and Harry Porter told him in confidence that the Duke of Suffolk has bought the right of one Brytyeff, which makes a claim on Hellesdon, and the said Duke intends to take possession within a short time after Easter. Because the said Russe understood from the said Barker and Porter that all the trustees will convey their estates to the Duke and do everything in their power to help him, in order to have his patronage.

Also, if it would please you, it seems to me that you need to send us word what arrangements to make for your old malt, because if any hot weather comes after it has lain there over the winter season it will be lost unless it is sold soon. Because regarding the price here, it has fallen badly. I have sold 100 coombs[73] of malt that came from Guton to James Golbeter, freed from refuse and level measured,[74] for 2s 2d per coomb, and to be paid at Midsummer and Lammas.

Also, there are several of your tenants' dwellings at Mautby which stand in great need of repair, and the tenants are so poor that they are not able to repair them. Therefore if it pleases you, I would like the marsh that Bridge had to remain under your own control this year, so that the tenants could have rushes to repair their houses with. And also there is windfall wood at the manor that is of no great value, which might help them with the repairs if it pleases you to let those in greatest need have it. I have said to Burgess that he should pay the value of the marsh, otherwise I told him that he could no longer have it, because you could find other lessees who would give what it was let for before. And if he would give for it as much as another man would, you would rather he had it than any other man. And he said he would give me an answer by a fortnight after Easter. I have found no other lessee for it yet.

Also, I understand from John Pamping[75] that you do not wish your son to be received into your house nor to be helped by you until the same time

---

[73] A coomb is a unit of measurement: 1 coomb equals 4 bushels.
[74] I have omitted the following phrase, which includes a word that appears in Davis as 'jument' ('a beast of burden') and in Gairdner's edition as 'inmet' ('the edible parts of an animal, entrails') because its meaning is unclear.
[75] Pamping was a Paston family servant, with whom Margaret's daughter Anne fell in love.

of year that he was put out of it last year, which will be about the time of the Translation of St Thomas. For God's sake, sir, have pity on him. And remember it has been a long time since he had anything from you to help him, and he has been obedient to you, and will be at all times, and will do all that he can and may to have your good fatherhood. And out of respect for God, be a good father and show some fatherly feeling towards him. And I believe he will be more aware of his own failings from now on, and be more careful to avoid the things that would displease you, and take heed of the things that would please you. Pecock[76] will tell you by mouth about more things than I can write to you about now.

May the blessed Trinity protect you. Written at Caister in haste on the first Monday after Palm Sunday.

Your M.P.

No. 43: Margaret Paston to John Paston I.

Margaret tells her husband that she plans to stake the Paston's claim to Hellesdon and Drayton. John II is due to return, and Margaret promises to keep a close eye on him.

[3 May 1465]

To my most honourable husband John Paston may this be delivered in haste.

Most honourable husband, I commend myself to you. May it please you to know that I have spoken to several of your tenants at Drayton this week, and encouraged them that everything will be well from now on, by the grace of God. And I understand from them that they will be very glad to have their old master back and this is so for all of them except for one or two who are dishonest villains.

And this next week I intend to go to Hellesdon on Wednesday or Thursday, and to stay there for a week or two and send our men out to collect money at Drayton and Hellesdon. And if you want I will have a manorial court held at Drayton before I leave there. I entreat you to send me word what you want me to do about it. I received two letters from you from Nicoll Colman yesterday, in which you request that we should make arrangements for your malt and barley, and we shall do so as best we can and send you word quickly of how we get on.

Also, yesterday Master Philip seized Dorlet's horse on Drayton land, when they were ploughing, for the whole year's lease of land. And, so I am told, the tenants of Drayton told him he did wrong him to make him pay for

---

76 William Pecock was another Paston family servant.

the whole year, because none of the tenants had paid him, except for the half. And he said that although they had only paid for the half, Paston should pay for the other half, and for more years also if he lived. But I expect to get Dorlet's horse back for him, or else Master Philip is likely to be un-horsed immediately, if we all live.

Your son will come home tomorrow, I believe, and I shall let you know how he conducts himself from now on. And I beg you do not think that I will support or favour him in any low behaviour, because I will not. I will let you know how I find him from now on. . . .

Written in haste at Caister on Holy Rood Day, etc. . . .

No. 44: Margaret Paston to John Paston I.

Margaret gives her husband a report about the escalating conflict over Drayton and Hellesdon, and informs him that she has made a complaint to the Bishop of Norwich. She explains that she is unable to leave Hellesdon and she has left John II in charge of Caister. Margaret advises her husband to avoid conflict with his own mother.

[10 May 1465]

To my master John Paston the eldest may this be delivered in haste.

Most honourable husband, I commend myself to you. May it please you to know that last Wednesday Daubeney, Naunton, Wykes and John Love were at Drayton to speak with your tenants there, to encourage them and also to ask for money from them. And Piers Warren, also known as Piers at Sloth – who is an unreliable fellow, and in with Master Philip and the bailiff of Costessey – he was ploughing your land in Drayton. And your said servants then seized his plough-team there, that is to say two mares, and brought them to Hellesdon, and they are still there. And the next morning, Master Philip and the bailiff of Costessey came to Hellesdon with a great number of people, that is to say eight score men and more in armour. And there they took two horses worth 4 marks from the parson's plough, and two horses worth 40 shillings from Thomas Stermyn's plough, saying to them that there was a charge against them in the hundred court brought by the said Piers for seizing the aforementioned plough-team at Drayton. And unless they would undertake on oath to come to Drayton next Tuesday to answer such matters as will be put to them there, they would not get their beasts back; which they refused to do until such time as they had an answer from you. And so they took the beasts away to Drayton, and from Drayton to Costessey.

And on the afternoon of the same day, the parson of Hellesdon sent his man to Drayton with Stermyn to speak with Master Philip, to find out if there was a way they could have their cattle back or not. And Master Philip answered them that if they would return the distrained property that was taken from Piers Warren, then he would give them theirs, otherwise not. And he let them know plainly that if you or any of your servants distrained anything in Drayton, even if it were only the value of a hen, they would come to Hellesdon and there seize the value of an ox for it. And if they cannot seize the value of that from there, that then they will break into your tenants' houses in Hellesdon, and seize as much as they can find inside. And if they were stopped in that – which it will never be in your power to do, 'because the Duke of Suffolk is able to maintain in his house every day more men than Daubeney has hairs on his head, if he likes, and as for Daubeney, he is a foolish fellow, and he shall be treated as such in future, and I wish he was here' – and therefore, he said, if you undertake to stop them doing so, that then they would go into any property that you had in Norfolk and Suffolk and distrain just as they would in Hellesdon. And they could get no other answer, and so they left.

Richard Calle asked the parson and Stermyn if they would take legal action over their cattle, and the parson said he was old and infirm and he did not want to be troubled with it. He said he would rather lose his cattle, because he knew very well that if he did do so he would be indicted and so vexed by them that he would never have any peace because of them. As for Stermyn, he said at that time that he dared not take out a suit against them either. But after Richard had gone I spoke with him, and he said he would be governed by your wishes, and I found him very loyal and well disposed in that businesss. . . .

Skipwith went with me to the Bishop of Norwich, and I informed him of Master Philip's riotous and evil disposition – asking his lordship to see if a means of correction might be found, given that he was chief justice of the peace, and his ordinary, and given that he was a priest and subject to his correction – so that he might have an understanding of his disposition. And I got Daubeney to tell him all about this business. And he said he would send for him and speak to him. And he told me several things about his conduct from which I understood that he did not like his disposition or his conduct in this business or in any other, because it seemed he had revealed himself for what he is in other matters.

My lord said to me that he would be very glad if you had a good result in your business. And he said that on his word of honour he favoured you, and would be very glad if you came home. And he said to me that that would be a great encouragement to your friends and neighbours, and that your presence should do more for them than a hundred of men should in your absence, and your enemies would be afraid to act against you if you were at home and moving amongst them. And he talked very openly about many other things that it would take too long to write about now, as Skipwith will tell you when he comes to you.

I entreat you to thank Skipwith for his support, because he was more than willing to go with me and give me his advice. It seems to me that he is very well disposed towards you.

Also, I entreat you to send me word quickly how you want us to be guided with this place, because I am told that it is soon likely to be as much at risk as the other is. On Thursday, for the whole day, there were as many as 60 people kept in Drayton lodge, and I have been told that there are still about 16 or 20 people inside day and night.

Also, I am told that Thomas Ellis, who has now been chosen as mayor, said at Drayton that if my lord of Suffolk needed a hundred men, he would provide them. And if any men in the town wanted to go to Paston, he would have them put in prison at once. I wish your men could get a *supersedeas* from the Chancery Court and be out of the power of their men here, and I beg you do not let Will Naunton be forgotten in this. Richard Calle and others can tell you of his conduct, and I beg you not to be displeased about him staying with me, because in good faith he has been a great help to me since you left here, as I will let you know in the future. I beg you, if his brother comes to you for a release of his land, not to let him have it until you see his father's will, the whereabouts of which I know, and may it please you to ask him to be a good brother to him.

Also, I have left John Paston the elder at Caister to look after the property there, as Richard will be able to tell you, because I would rather, if it pleased you, be captainess here than at Caister. Yet I had no intention of staying here when I left home for more than a day or two, but I shall stay here until I hear tidings from you.

Also, I am told that the Duke of Suffolk has bought, or will quickly buy, the right that a certain Brytyeff has in Hellesdon, etc. . . .

Also, my mother told me that she considers it very odd that she cannot get the profits of Clere's property in a peaceful fashion because of you. She says it is hers and she has still paid most for it, and she says she wants to have the profits from it, or else she will make more people speak of it. She says she knows of no claim or legal right you have concerning it, unless you want a dispute with her, which will not earn you any respect. And she says she will be there this summer and repair the housing there. In good faith, I hear much talk of the conduct between you and her. I would be very glad, and so would many more of your friends, if things were different between you than they are, and if they were I believe you would have better success in other business.

I pray that God will help you in all your business, and give you grace to have a good result in it soon, because this is too wearying a life to endure for you and all your people. Written in haste at Hellesdon on 10th May. The reason that I write to you in haste is to have an answer from you in haste. Yours, M.P.

No. 45: Margaret Paston to John Paston I.

Margaret informs her husband that she had their men seize cattle in lieu of rent, but was forced to return the animals after two days.

[20 May 1465]

To my most honourable husband John Paston may this be delivered in haste.

May it please you to know that last Saturday your servants Naunton, Wykes and others were at Drayton, and there they distrained for the rent and payment that was owed to the value of seventy-seven cattle. And they brought them home to Hellesdon and put them in the pound, and kept them there from the said Saturday morning until Monday at 3 o'clock in the afternoon. At first, on that same Saturday, the tenants followed and wanted to have their cattle back, and I answered that if they would pay the charges that they ought to pay to you then they would have their cattle given back. Otherwise, if they were unable to pay ready money, then they should find sufficient surety to pay the money on such a day as they might agree with me, and be bound to you for it in a bond. And they said they dared not undertake to be bound, and as for money they had none to pay at that time, and therefore I kept the beasts. Harleston was in Norwich and sent for the tenants on that Saturday afternoon. And there, with the help of the bailiff of Costessey, he made the tenants very afraid, saying that if they would pay such charges or be bound to pay, they would turn them out of the lands they held in bond from the Duke of Suffolk. And they would distrain and dispute with them so that they for their part would be weary, and they would make them so afraid they would not dare pay or be bound. And on the same day at the time of evensong Harleston came to me at Hellesdon, requesting me to return the distrained property, and, if I did, the distrained property they had taken from your tenants would be given back in the same way. And I said I would not give them back, and told them I would give them back on the terms which you wrote previously, and otherwise not; and otherwise I would not give them back except by due process of law. And we discussed several other matters at that time, which would take too long to write about now, but you will be informed about it very soon.

And on the following Monday at 9 o'clock Pinchmore came to Hellesdon with a *replevin* which was made in Harleston's name as under-steward of the

Duchy[77] saying that the beasts were taken from Duchy lands. Therefore he requested me to release to him the animals that were taken in this way, and I said I would not give them back until such time as I had examined the tenants for the truth. And so I sent Wykes and Pinchmore there to find out what they would say. And the tenants said that to their knowledge none were taken from the Duchy lands, except for the younger Piers Warren and Painter who said their cattle were taken from Duchy lands, which they cannot prove with any witnesses except their own words. And so we were not willing to obey that *replevin*, and so they went away. And at 3 o'clock in the afternoon Pinchmore came to Hellesdon again with two men whose names are John Whycherly and Robert Ranson who brought with them a *replevin* from the sheriff, which writ required me to hand over those beasts seized at Drayton. And so I, seeing the sheriff's *replevin* sealed with his seal, ordered my men to hand them over, and so they were returned.

And as for all the other business you have written to me about, I will hasten to send you an answer in as much haste as I can, because I do not have time to write any more to you now.

May the Blessed Trinity protect you. Written at Hellesdon on 20th May. By yours, M.P.

No. 46: Margaret Paston to John Paston I.

Margaret Paston tells her husband that that the tenants have pledged their allegiance to them, and asks for advice about how to proceed in the shire court. Margaret also proposes a secret visit to her husband.

[27 May 1465]

To my most honourable husband John Paston may this be delivered in haste.

Most honourable husband, I commend myself to you. . . .

I have not spoken with my mother since Richard Calle brought me the letter from you regarding her business, because I could not find time. When I find time to speak with her I will remind her about that business as you directed in your letter. And as for your tenants in Drayton, I understand from them that they are very well disposed and as loyal to you as it is in their power to be, and would be very glad if you had it back peaceably. Because they would almost rather be the Devil's tenants than the Duke's,

---

[77] The Duchy of Lancaster.

except for Will Hearn, Piers at Sloth and one Knott from the same town, because they are not good. All your tenants at Hellesdon and Drayton except these three are very glad that we are there amongst them, and so are many others of our old neighbours and friends.

And unless you come home by Wednesday or Thursday in Whitsun Week, I intend to see you by secret means by Trinity Sunday, unless you send me orders to the contrary before that time. . . .

And may the Blessed Trinity protect you. Written the first Monday after Ascension Day.

By yours, M.P.

No. 47: Margaret Paston to John Paston III.

In this, her first surviving letter to John III, Margaret writes to him regarding arrangements for his sister Margery. John III had been in the service of the Duke of Norfolk for the past three years.

[Probably 30 June 1465]

To John Paston the younger.

I greet you warmly, letting you know that regarding your sister's being with my lady, if your father will agree to it, I consider myself very well pleased. Because I would be very glad for her to do her service rather than anyone else, if she were able to do what should please my lady's good grace. Therefore I would like you to speak to your father about it, and let him know that I am pleased for her to go there if he is. Because I would be very glad if she could be offered in marriage or in service in a way that would be to her honour and profit in repaying her friends. And I entreat you to do your part in this for your own honour and hers.

And as soon as you can do so without difficulty, arrange for me to have back the 6 marks you know about, for I would not like your father to know about it.

Also, if you pass through London send me back my chain, and the little chain I lent you previously, by some trustworthy person. And if you want my good wishes avoid such things I spoke to you about last time in our parish church.

I pray that God will make you as virtuous a man as any of your kin has ever been, and that you may have God's blessing and mine, in order that you do well etc. Written the first Sunday after you left. And I beg you send me some tidings as soon as you can once you get to London about how your father and brother are getting on with their affairs.

By your mother.

No. 48: Margaret Paston to John Paston II.

Margaret Paston writes to her eldest son at Hellesdon, warning him that the Duke of Suffolk is likely to attack, and instructing him to prepare for this eventuality.

[Perhaps 6 July 1465]

I greet you warmly, letting you know that I am reliably informed that the Duke of Suffolk is building up a large force in both Norfolk and Suffolk to come down with him and drive us back, if they can. Therefore I want you to use any means to make yourself as secure as you can in the place. Because I and many others believe that if they do not find you here they will look for you where you are. I would like John Paston the younger to ride back to my lady of Norfolk, and stay with her until we have other news. And he may do some good there, once he hears news, by going on to his father or to some other place where we may get relief from trouble. Because I am told that more than 200 men have come to Costessey, and it is said that there are more than a thousand coming. I would like you to send Little John here so that I can send him out on my errands. Let me know how you are doing by one of the tenants who will not be recognised.

Also, order Richard Calle to send me word by letter of how many of the matters – which my husband, in the various letters he sent home, asked to be advanced here – he has sent him an answer to; and of the lessees of Titchwell.

Also, if Sir James Gloys can come to Adam Taylor's house in Norwich, I would like him to come early on Monday, and I shall contact him there.

May God protect you all. Written in haste on Saturday.

By your mother.

Also, I have been told that Heydon is rousing many people in the soke and in other places.

Also, I want you to hurry Richard Calle in making up the accounts, and if he needs it, let him get help. And keep Thomas Hunworth with you for now. And beware of theft.

No. 49: Margaret Paston to John Paston I.

Margaret informs her husband that the Duke of Suffolk, along with his mother and wife, are coming to Costessey, and asks how he wants her to proceed.

[12 July 1465]

To my most honourable husband John Paston, in haste.

Most honourable husband, I commend myself to you, entreating you with all my heart that you will seek a way for your servants to live in peace, because they are in fear of their lives every day. The Duke of Suffolk's men daily threaten Daubeney, Wykes and Richard Calle, saying that wherever they can find them they will die. And assaults have been made on Richard Calle this week, so that he was at great risk from them in Norwich. And great assaults were made on me and my company here last Monday, about which Richard Calle tells me he has sent you word in writing more openly than I can do at this time, but I shall inform you more openly in the future.

I believe there will be a major initiative against you and your servants at the assizes and sessions here, therefore it seems to me, unless you give better advice, that it would be best if you were to speak to the justices before they come here. And if you want me to complain to them or anyone else, if God grants me life and health, I will do as you advise me to do, because in good faith I have been poorly treated by them. And what with the illness and distress that I have had, I am feeling very low and weak, but I will do all that is in my power to do in your affairs.

The Duke of Suffolk and both the Duchesses are coming to Claxton today, so I am informed, and next week he will be at Costessey. Whether he will come nearer here or not I do not know yet. It is said that he might come here, and yet his men said here on Monday that he did not claim any right to this place. They said they were coming only to seize those people who are riotous in this place, and those who are the King's felons and indicted and outlawed men. Nevertheless, they would not show any warrants empowering them to seize such people, even if there had been any here. I believe that if they were coming in peace, they would have given another reason for coming. When it was all over and they were leaving, Harleston and others asked me to come and see my old lady,[78] and petition the Duke, and if anything was wrong it would be put right. I said if I was going to appeal for any redress I would appeal to a higher authority, and let the King and all the lords of this land know what has been done to us, if the Duke would stand by what has been done to us by his servants, if you would give me permission. I entreat you to send me word if you want me to make any complaint to the Duke or the Duchess. Because I have been told they do not know the plain truth about the things that have been done in their names. I would write much more to you were it not for lack of time.

I ordered my Master Tom to return to me from Norwich after he had spoken with Richard Calle, but he did not come. I wish he were free of his indictment, provided that he were free of your service. Because on my word of honour I consider the place where he is to be the more ill-favoured because of his disposition in various things, which you will be informed about in the future.

[78] The dowager Duchess.

May the Trinity protect you. Written the first Friday after St Thomas' Day. By your M.P.

No. 50: Margaret Paston to John Paston I.

Margaret informs her husband that she and her men had been frustrated in their attempts to hold a manorial court at Drayton, but that, despite the accusations made against her and her men, she received a sympathetic hearing at the assize. She tells him of her fears that she will be attacked at Hellesdon.

[7 August 1465]

To my most honourable husband John Paston may this be delivered in haste.

Most honourable husband, I commend myself to you. May it please you to know that on Lammas Day I sent Thomas Bond and Sir James Gloys to Drayton to hold the manorial court in your name and claim your right of possession, because I could not get anyone else to hold the court, nor to go there except the said Thomas Bond. Because I believe they were afraid of the people who would be there on the Duke of Suffolk's behalf. The said Thomas and James met the Duke of Suffolk's men – that is to say Harleston, the parson of Sall Master Philip, and William Yelverton,[79] who was steward, with an estimated 60 or more people, and the tenants of the same town, some of them carrying rusty pole-axes and billhooks – as they came into the manor yard to hold the court, and told them they had come to hold the court in your name and to claim your right of possession. At this the said Harleston, without any more words or cause given by your men, committed the said Thomas Bond into the custody of the new bailiff of Drayton, William Docket, saying that he should go to my lord and deliver the message himself, even though it was Sir James who delivered the message and had been the spokesperson. And thus they seized the said Thomas without cause. They wanted to make out that the said Thomas had been spokesperson, and the said James told them that he was spokesperson, because he was the more peaceable man. Afterwards they ordered him to go away and then led Thomas Bond away to Costessey, and bound his arms behind him with whipcord like a thief, and would have taken him to the Duke of Suffolk if I had not spoken to the judges in the morning before they went to the shire house and informed them about the riots and assaults they had made on me and my men.

---

[79] William Yelverton II, the son of William Yelverton I.

The bailiff of Costessey and all the Duke of Suffolk's council being present there and all the learned men of Norfolk, and William Jenney and many people from the locality, the judge calling the bailiff of Costessey to come before them all, he rebuked him in strong terms, commanding the sheriff to see what force they had gathered at Drayton. Afterwards he came to Hellesdon to see the forces there, and he was very satisfied with the force. And from there he rode to Drayton to see people there who had been taken away before he arrived, and there he asked for Thomas Bond to be handed over to him. And they begged for pardon and said that they had sent him to the Duke of Suffolk. Nevertheless they afterwards sent him to him in Norwich, asking him not to hand him over without fining him for disrupting the King's court. . . . And in good faith I found the judges very gracious and patient with me in my business, despite the Duke's counsel having made their complaint to them before I came, in the worst way, accusing us of gathering a large force and of many riotous things done by me and your men. And after I had informed the judges of their dishonesty and their conduct, and of our own conduct in the same way, and when the judge understood the truth, he rebuked the bailiff of Costessey in the strongest terms in front of me and many others, saying that unless he improved his disposition and behaviour they would inform the King and help to get him punished.

And although you advised me to [gather[80]] a body of men to hold the court at Drayton at a moderate cost, your counsel thought it would be better to do otherwise and not to gather a force, because I was told that the Duke's men numbered 500 men. And your counsel advised me to get a body of men to protect my property at Hellesdon, because I was told that they would come and drag me out of the property, which made me guard the place more securely at that time.

And as for holding any court for you at Drayton, I do not see now it could be brought about without the help of others, without great inconvenience resulting from it. . . .

Also, next Tuesday, the sessions of the peace will be held at Walsingham. What will be done there I still do not know, because regarding any indictments that we try to bring against them, it is only a waste of work as neither the sheriff nor the jurors will do anything against them. . . .

I entreat you to send me word what I should do in this business and in everything else, etc. And may God protect you. Written in haste the first Wednesday after Lammas Day.

Your M. PASTON.

---

[80] Word obliterated by torn edge.

No. 51: Margaret Paston to John Paston I.

Margaret expresses her concern that her last letter to her husband may have gone astray, and updates him about the proceedings in various courts. Norwich is host to the plague, and there is news of another death. Margaret tells her husband that she hopes to see him in person but arrangements need to be made for the safety of their property. She also intercedes with her husband on Elizabeth Clere's behalf, following a disagreement.

[18 August 1465]

To my most honourable master John Paston may this letter be delivered in haste.

Most honourable husband, I commend myself to you. May it please you to know that I received a letter from you sent by Laurence Reed last Friday, from which I understand that you had had no tidings from me at the time your letter was written, which I am surprised about, because I sent you a letter by Chittock's son, who is an apprentice in London, which was given to him the first Thursday after Lammas Day. And he promised to set off the same day and that you would have it as quickly as possible after he arrived in London. And the said letter concerned the proceedings of the assizes in Norwich and various other matters. I entreat you to let me know if you have it. As for the *replevins*, Richard Calle says he has sent you an answer about them, and also copies of them. As for the high sheriff, he conducted himself very well here towards me, and he told me that as for the *replevins* he would take advice of learned men as to what he could do. And he will act towards you and yours as generously as he can in this and in any other matter concerning you, without loss to himself.

The reason I did not write to you before I did after the sessions was because Yelverton held sessions at Dereham and Walsingham the week following the assizes, in order to find out what was undertaken there and send you word of it. Great efforts were made by the bailiff of Costessey and others to have indicted your men, both at Dereham and at Walsingham, but I found a way to stop their plans on those two occasions. I sent Richard Calle to Sir Thomas Howes yesterday, about my lady Bedford's business, but he has been unable to speak with him, and I have still not received an answer, but I will send a message to him again this week. . . .

Master John Eastgate passed to God last Thursday, may God absolve his soul; about which in good faith I am very sad, because I found him very loyal to you. They die in agony in Norwich. . . .

Also, as for my coming to you, if it would please you for me to come I believe I shall manage to arrange everything before I come so that it will be safe enough, by the grace of God, until I come home again. But out of respect for God, if you can, arrange a way to come home yourself, because that would be most profitable to you, because here people cut large thongs from other people's leather. I shall write to you again as quickly as I can.

May God protect you. Written in haste at Hellesdon the first Sunday after the Assumption of Our Lady.

Also, my cousin, Elizabeth Clere is at Ormesby, and your mother proposes to be at her house at Caister this week, because the plague is so rampant in Norwich that they dare no longer stay there. May God help us, I understand from your mother that she would be very glad if you did well, and had great success in all your affairs. And I understand from my cousin Clere that she would be glad to have your good will and she has sworn sincerely to me that no fault will be found in her, nor has there been, if the truth were known, as she believes it will be in the future. She says there is no man alive that she has put her trust in as much as she has done in you. She says she well knows that the sort of talk about her that has been reported, which has been other than she deserves, causes you to act differently towards her than you should. She told me this weeping, and told me of several other things that you will know of in the future.

By yours, M.P.

No. 52: Margaret Paston to John Paston I.

Margaret writes a letter of encouragement to her husband, suggesting that she visit him in London, where he was imprisoned in the Fleet.

[Probably August 1465]

Most honourable husband, I commend myself to you and entreat you with all my heart out of respect for God to be encouraged and trust in the grace of God that you will overcome your enemies and your troublesome business completely, if you will be encouraged and not take your problems so sorrowfully that you harm yourself. And believe truly that you are strong enough for all your enemies, by the grace of God. Your mother is your good mother and takes your business to heart. And if you think that I might do any good in your business if I come up to see you, once I know your intentions, it will not be long before I am with you, by the grace of God. And as for any other things of importance in this locality, I believe I shall arrange it so it will be safe. I have given your elder son 20 marks that I received from Richard Calle, and I have been unable to get any more from him since you left.

And I entreat God with all my heart to send us tidings about you, and grant you victory over your enemies.

Written in haste on Saturday.

Yours, M.P.

Also, I am giving your son 10 marks of your father's small change that was in the chest, because my brother Clement says that 20 marks was too little for him.

No. 53: Margaret Paston to John Paston I.[81]

Having visited her husband in prison, Margaret writes to him informing him of a successful attempt to prevent rival claimants holding a manor-ial court at Caldecott. Cotton was a former Fastolf manor which, a few years previously, William Yelverton I and his associate William Jenney had seized and sold to Gilbert Debenham, who also asserted ownership of Caldecott.

[27 September 1465]

Most honourable husband, I commend myself to you, wishing with all my heart to hear of your health and happiness, thanking you for the warm welcome you gave me and for the amount you spent on me. You spent more than I wished you to, unless it pleased you to do so. May God give me grace to do what would please you.

May it please you to know that on Friday after I left you I was at Sudbury, and spoke with the sheriff, and Richard Calle took him the two writs. And he broke them open, and Richard has the copies of them. And he said he would send the writs to his undersheriff, and a letter with them requiring him to act as generously as he ought to do in this. And I and Richard informed him of the conduct of his undersheriff, how partial he had been towards the other party both in that business and also in the actions in the shire courts. And he was not at all pleased about the conduct of his undersheriff, and he has written to him that he ought to be impartial to both parties as the law requires, both in that business and in all other. What the undersheriff will do about it I do not know, because he has not yet been spoken with.

Also, as for Cotton, I took possession of the place last Sunday and I stayed there until last Wednesday. I have left there the younger John Paston, Wykes and twelve other men, to collect the profits of the manor. And by the day the court will be held, I believe there will be more to reinforce them if necessary. John Paston has been with my lord of Norfolk since we took possession, and requested his support to provide reinforcements with the

---

[81] No address or signature.

men of his household and others if necessary, and he has promised he would do so. And on Tuesday I sent Richard Calle to Knyvett, asking him to send a message to his bailiff and tenants at Mendlesham that they should be ready to come to John Paston when he sent for them. And he sent one of his men straightaway, ordering them to do so by whatever means. And he sent me a message by Richard, and his son too, that if we were not strong enough either he or his son, or both if need be, would come with whatever body of men they could gather, and that they would act as loyally as they could for you, both in that business and in all other.

Also, last Saturday, Jenney gave notice in Caldecott of a manorial court to be held there last Tuesday in his name, and, on the Sunday after, Debenham gave notice of another court to be held there in his name the same Tuesday. And Daubeney knew about it and he sent a message to your elder son on Sunday night to get some men from there, and so he sent Wykes and Berney to him on Monday morning. And as soon as they got to Caister they sent for men in the district there, and so they got three score men. And Daubeney and Wykes and Berney rode to Caldecott that same Monday night with their body of men and kept them secretly in the place so that none of the tenants knew they were there except Rising's wife and her household until 10 o' clock on Tuesday. And then Sir Thomas Brews, Debenham the father, and his son the knight, Jenney, Micklefield, young Jermyn and young Jerningham, and the bailiff of Mutford, with others numbering three score people who came from the sessions at Beccles which had been held there the day before, came to St Olaf's. And they remained there and dined, and when they had dined Sir Gilbert Debenham came to Caldecott with twenty horsemen to find out what the forces were in the place. And then Wykes saw them coming, and he and Berney with two others rode out to speak to them. And when Sir Gilbert saw them coming, he and his force fled and rode back to St Olaf's. And then they sent young Jerningham and the bailiff of Mutford to your men, letting them know that the justice of the peace had come down with Debenham and Jenney to ensure that the peace was kept, and that they were able to enter and hold the court in a peaceful manner. And your men answered and said that they knew no one possessed it, nor any right to it except you, and so they said they would hold it in your name and according to your right. And so they went back again with this answer, and they were frustrated in their intentions that day. And all the tenants' animals were driven off Caldecott fee, and will be until other redress may be had. Your men did not want to hold a court there that day because the other party had given notice of it, but we will give notice of a court and hold it, I believe, very soon. You will laugh to hear the outcome of the action there, which would be too long to write about at the moment. Berney will tell you when he comes to you, but he will not come to you till after St Faith's Mass, so that he can bring you answers about other business.

I am told the sessions will be here in Norwich next Tuesday, and in Suffolk the sessions shall be the same Tuesday either at Dunwich or at Ipswich. I expect there will be initiatives against some of our people there, but we shall try to frustrate their intentions if we can. I am told that had there been no people left here in this place while I was away there would have been a new master here by now. Therefore it is still not a good idea to leave it unattended.

Also, Arblaster has sent a letter to my lord of Oxford's tenants who are nearest to Cotton asking them to help John Paston if they are requested to, etc. . . .

Also, I have asked about your worsted[82] but you cannot have it until All Souls Day, and then I have been promised that you will have the finest that can be made. Richard Calle will bring it up with him.

Written the Friday before Michaelmas Day.

No. 54: Margaret Paston to John Paston I.

Following an attack on October 15ᵗʰ, when the Duke of Suffolk's forces destroyed the manor house and neighbouring buildings at Hellesdon and looted items from the church, Margaret Paston writes to her husband describing what has taken place and requesting instructions about how to proceed.

[17 October 1465]

On Tuesday morning John Butler, otherwise called John Palmer, and Davy Arnold your cook, and William Malthouse of Aylsham were seized at Hellesdon by the bailiff of Eye, called Bottesforth, and taken away to Costessey. And they are imprisoning them there still, without a warrant or any authority of a justice of the peace. And they say they will take them to Eye prison, and as many of your men and tenants they can get whom they know support you or are on your side, they are threatened with slaying or imprisoning.

The Duke came to Norwich on Tuesday at 10 o'clock with five hundred men. And he sent for the mayor and alderman and the sheriffs, asking them in the King's name to make an inquiry of the constables in every ward within the city about which men would have joined your side to help or aid your men at any time during these gatherings, and if they could find any, they should seize and arrest them and punish them, and also confirm the names to him on Wednesday by 8 o'clock, which the mayor did. And he will do anything he can for him and his. And following this the mayor has arrested one who was with

---

[82] A fine wool fabric, here referring to a doublet which John Paston I previously requested to have made.

me called Robert Lovegold, a brass-worker, and threatened to hang him by the neck. Therefore I would like a writ sent down to remove him, if you think it should be done. He was not with me, not except when Harleston and the others made the attack on me at Lammas. He is very true and loyal to you, and therefore I want him to be helped. I have no man to wait upon me at this time who will dare take sides except Little John. William Naunton is here with me, but he dare not take sides because he is greatly threatened. I am told the old lady and the Duke are set fervently against us by the information of Harleston, the bailiff of Costessey, and Andrews, and Dogget the bailiff's son, and other such dishonest villains who would like this business carried through to their own satisfaction; which causes evil gossip in this area and other places.

And as for Sir John Heveningham, Sir John Wingfield, and other honourable men, they have only been made their tools, which I believe will discredit them in future. I spoke with Sir John Heveningham and informed him of the truth of the matter, and of all our conduct at Drayton. And he said he wanted everything to be well, and he would tell my lord, but Harleston had all the influence and power with the Duke, and he followed his advice and Dr Aleyn's here now.

The lodge and the remainder of your house was broken down on Tuesday and Wednesday, and on Wednesday the Duke rode to Drayton and then on to Costessey, while the lodge at Hellesdon was being broken down. And tonight at midnight Thomas Sleaford, Green, Porter and the bailiff of Eye and others got a cart and took away feather beds and all our possessions that were left for safeguarding at the parson's and Thomas Water's house. I shall send you lists before long detailing as accurately as I can the possessions we have lost. I entreat you to let me know how you want me to proceed, whether you want me to stay at Caister or come to you in London.

I have no time to write any more. May God protect you. Written at Norwich on St Luke's Eve.

M.P.

No. 55: Margaret Paston to John Paston I.

Margaret informs her husband that the attack on Hellesdon has generated support for him in the area, and she describes the crowds of sightseers coming to view the destruction. She also tells him that she is weary of all the trouble.

[27 October 1465]

To my most honourable husband John Paston may this be delivered in haste.

Most honourable husband, I commend myself to you. . . .

Bartholomew White has been treated with hostility, and his brother, and others who came with him to bear witness, and they were beaten and put in prison and shamefully abused by Harleston and others of the Duke of Suffolk's men. Unless the things they have done can be soon corrected people think that they will soon do more harm. I was at Hellesdon last Thursday, and saw the place, and in good faith no one could imagine what a bad and horrible state it is in unless they saw it. Many people come every day out of curiosity, from both Norwich and other places, and say it is a shame. It would have been better for the Duke not to have done this than to have £1000, and you have the good will of the people because it is so evilly done. And they made your tenants from Hellesdon and Drayton, with others, help to break down the walls of both the house and the lodge, entirely against their wills, God knows, but through fear they dared not do otherwise. I have spoken with your tenants both at Hellesdon and Drayton, and reassured them as well as I can.

The Duke's men ransacked the church and took away all the goods that were left there, both of ours and of the tenants, and did not leave much. But they stood on the high altar and ransacked the images, and took away whatever they could find, and forced the parson out of the church until they had finished, and ransacked the houses of everyone in the town five or six times. And the chief leaders of the robbery were the bailiff of Eye, the bailiff of Stradbroke, and Thomas Sleaford. And Sleaford was the chief robber of the church, and next to the bailiff of Eye he has most of the plunder. And as for lead, brass, pewter, iron, doors, gates, and other possessions from the house, men from Costessey and Cawston have it, and what they could not carry they have hacked apart in the most malicious manner. If it could be arranged, I would like some honourable men to be sent from the King to see what it is like, both there and at the lodge, before any snows come, so that they can bear witness to the truth. Otherwise it will not be seen as clearly as it can be now.

And out of respect for God, advance your business now, because the cost and trouble we have daily now, and shall have until things are different, are too horrible. And your men dare not go about gathering rent, and we keep more than three hundred people here every day to protect us and the house, because, in all faith, if the place had not been strongly protected the Duke would have come here.

The mayor of Norwich arrested the bailiff of Normand's, Lovegold, Gregory Cordoner, and Bartholomew Fuller without any authority except he says he had an order from the Duke to do so. And he will not let them out of prison until he has surety of £80 for each of them to answer whatever matters the Duke and his counsel will put to them whenever they are called. And he will do the same to others, as many as he can get, who show you any good will. And also the mayor would have them swear they would never act against the Duke or any of his supporters, which they would in no way do. Poor Bartholomew remains there due to lack of surety. He was formerly of much service to Edmund Clere. Arblaster thinks that Hugh at Fen could be a great help in your affairs, and he thinks he will act loyally, if you wish, etc.

Out of respect for God, if any honourable and profitable way can be found in your business to free us from our trouble and great costs and expenses that we have and which may grow in future, do not neglect it. It is thought here that if my lord of Norfolk would take up your cause, and get a commission to inquire into the riots and robberies that have been inflicted upon you and others in the district, then all the district will wait on him and serve your purpose. Because the people love and fear him more than any other lord except the King and my lord of Warwick, etc. . . .

And I entreat you with all my heart to send me word in haste how you are doing, and how you are getting on in your affairs, and to let me know how your sons are doing. I came home late tonight, and shall be here until I hear other news from you. Wykes came home on Saturday but he did not see your sons.

May God protect you, and send us good news from you. Written in a haste on the Eve of the Feast of St Simon and St Jude.
By yours, M.P.

No. 56: Margaret Paston to either John Berney or William Yelverton.[83]

Margaret writes requesting the release of the parson of Brandeston, who has been captured, and the return of her property that has been seized. If the letter is to Berney, the reference to illegal activities in the past is probably an allusion to his alleged involvement in a murder some years earlier.

[1466 or 1467]

Cousin, I commend myself to you, letting you know that I am informed that the parson of Brandeston has been seized by your soldiers and taken away with them, and they have rifled his goods and some of mine and my husband's as well, and those of his bailiff, which were left with the said parson to look after. Therefore I recommend and entreat

---

[83] No address or signature. Colin Richmond queries Davis' assumption that this letter is to John Berney and presents a strong case for Yelverton as an alternative candidate: *The Paston Family in the Fifteenth Century: Endings* (Manchester, Manchester University Press, 2000), pp.95–96 n.25. Richmond also suggests a later dating than that proposed by Davis (before May 1466).

that he may be let go again, and our goods that were taken from him be given back. Because, if your soldiers are of such a disposition that they will take what they can get, it will not gain you any honour or profit in the future, and I would be sorry about that. And if the said parson is not conducting himself as he ought to, I will help to see him punished as conscience and the law requires. I would like you to remember that you have taken the blame before for such things that have not been done as the law required.

And may God protect you. Written at Norwich.

No. 57: Margaret Paston to John Paston II.

Some months after the death of his father in May 1466, Margaret writes to her eldest son exhorting him to safeguard his documents.

[29 October 1466]

To my honourable master Sir John Paston, knight, may this letter be delivered in haste.

I greet you warmly, and send you God's blessing and mine, requesting you to send me word how you are getting on in your business, because it seems a very long time since I heard news from you. And I advise you always to be careful to guard your important documents wisely, so that they do not fall into the hands of those who could do you harm in the future. Your father, may God absolve him, in his troubled period set greater store by his documents and deeds than he did by any of his moveable goods. Remember that if those were taken from you, you could never get any more that would be of such help to you as those are, etc.

Also, I would like you to take heed that if any legal action is undertaken against me, or against any of those who were indicted before the coroner, that I might be informed about it, and to provide redress for it.

Also, as for your father's will, I would like you to take very good advice about it, as I am informed that it can be proved even if nobody takes responsibility for the administration this year. . . .

And, out of respect for God, progress your business now so that we may be at peace in the future, and do not give up now because of difficulty. And remember the great cost and responsibility we have had on this account, and truly believe it cannot last much longer. You know what you left when you were last at home, and know this truly, there is no more in this district with which to bear any expenses. I advise you to enquire wisely if you can get any more there where you are, because otherwise, by my faith, I fear things will not be well with us. And send me word soon how you are, and whether you have the last deeds that you were lacking, because clearly they are not in this district. I am told in private that Richard Calle has nearly won over your Uncle Will with kind promises regarding his property and other things, which should benefit him greatly, so he says. Take my advice and be wary of him and his companions.

May God send you much success in all your business. Written the morning after the Feast of St Simon and St Jude, at Caister, where I would not be now except for your sake, as I may prosper.
By your mother.

No. 58: Margaret Paston to John Paston II.

A couple of years later, William Yelverton I and other executors of Fastolf's will enfeoffed the Duke of Norfolk in the manor at Caister. Margaret informs her eldest son that Yelverton and his son and their agents had begun seizing animals and harassing tenants at Guton, and requests his help resolving the dispute. She alludes to John II's engagement to Anne Haute, a cousin of the Queen, and warns him against committing himself too hastily.

[12 March 1469]

To Sir John Paston, knight, may this be delivered in haste.

I greet you warmly and send you God's blessing and mine, wishing you to commend me to my brother William, and to discuss with him and your advisors the matters I am writing about, so that documentation from the King can be provided, so that the Duke of Norfolk and his advisors will cease the destruction they are doing on your estates, and especially at Hainford. Because they have felled all the wood and this week they will take it away, and let the water out and take all the fish. And Sir William Yelverton and his son William, John Grey, and Burgess, Will Yelverton's men, have been at Guton and seized property, and unless they pay them, they cannot set a plough to till their land. They tell them to leave their land uncultivated unless they pay them. If the tenants have no redress – so that they can harrow their land freely and in peace within seven days, without assault or distraint by Yelverton and his men or any others acting in their names – their cultivation of the fields will be lost for the whole year and they will be ruined. And even though you might keep it in peace in future, you would lose the rents for this year, because they cannot pay you unless they can use their land. They no sooner set a plough out of their gates than there is a band of men ready to seize it. And they ride with spears and lances like men of war, so that the said tenants are afraid to protect their own houses. Therefore provide a quick remedy or else you will lose the tenants' loyalty and you will suffer a great loss. Because it is a great pity to hear the shameful and piteous complaints from the poor tenants who come to me for support and help, sometimes six or seven together. Therefore, for the love of God, see that they are helped, and ask my brother, William, to give you good advice in this.

Also, I am told that my lady of Suffolk has promised you her support if your marriage arrangements stand, and to be as generous as is required or more so, if there is any agreement made regarding any business between you. If you are advised to pay her any money to make her refuse or disclaim her title of ownership, it seems to me you could excuse yourself due to the money she had before, and to the wrongs that were done by her men felling your wood and pulling down your house and lodge at Hellesdon, and seizing the sheep and your father's goods, which were seized when the said house was pulled down, for which, all things considered, she ought to recompense you. If the King and the lords were properly informed, they would more readily consider your losses. It seems this Sir William Yelverton has encouragement, that he is so bold, because he speaks in such a proud, rude way and is very insulting to the tenants, so they have reported to me. Therefore be very careful not to commit yourself nor make any engagement until you are sure of peaceful possession of your land. Because often haste brings regret, and when a man has made an agreement like that he must keep it, he has no choice in the matter. Do not be too hasty until your land is clear as to title. And work quickly towards a remedy in these matters, or else Sir John Fastolf's property, even if you take possession of it peacefully, will not be worth a groat[84] to you this year unless you are willing to ruin your tenants.

I beg you to remember a kerchief of cremil[85] for your sister Anne.

Remember to work towards some remedy concerning your father's will while my lord of Canterbury is alive, because he is an old man and he is now friendly towards you. And if he happened to die you never know who might come after him. And if he were a poor man he would be more difficult to deal with, because your father was rumoured to be so rich. And do not let this be forgotten about. Because if there was one who felt no good will towards us, he might call upon us to give an account of his property. And if we could not show why we have taken possession, he might pass a sentence excommunicating us in the diocese, and making us hand over his property, which would be very shameful

---

[84] A silver coin worth 4d.
[85] A fabric.

and a rebuke to us. Therefore, provide for this quickly and wisely while he is alive and do not delay as you did when my lord of York was chancellor. Because if you had made the effort in his time that you have since, this business would have been finished with. Guard against that, and do not let sloth catch you in this sort of negligence again. Think about the unfortunate consequences and have foresight in all your work, and you will do the better.

May God protect you. Written on Mid-Lent Sunday in haste.
By your mother, M.P.

No. 59: Margaret Paston to John Paston II.

Margaret urges John II to take his engagement seriously, and reiterates her advice about delaying marriage until the land disputes are resolved. She also entreats him to find a place for her daughter Margery, after relations between them had become strained.

[3 April 1469]

To Sir John Paston.

I greet you warmly, and send you God's blessings and mine, thanking you for sending me my seal. But I am really sorry you went to such expense for it, because one of a 40d would have done me very well. Let me know what it cost you and I will send you the money for it. I sent you a letter by a man from Yarmouth. Send me word if you have it, because I am surprised you sent me no answer to it with Juddy. I have no certain knowledge of your engagement, but, if you are engaged, I entreat God to send you joy and honour together, as I believe you will have if she is as she is reported to be. And in the sight of God you are as greatly committed to her as if you were married. And therefore, I order you upon my blessing to be as true to her as if she were actually married to you, and you will have more grace and better success in all other things. Also I would not like you to be too hasty to be married until you are more secure in your property, because you must remember what expense you will have; and if you have not the means to maintain it, it will be a great shame. And therefore work towards getting legal conveyances from the lords, and be more secure in your land before you are married.

The Duchess of Suffolk is at Ewelme in Oxfordshire, and your friends here think this has been done so that she might be far away, and more easily make excuses because of age or sickness if the King should send for her about your business.

Your enemies are as bold here as they were before. Therefore I can only think they have some encouragement. I sent a message to Caister that they should be careful in guarding the place, as you wrote to me. Make haste to resolve your business as swiftly as you can, so that you can keep a smaller body of men at Caister. Because the expenses and costs are great and you have no need of them if you remind yourself what other expenses you have and how your property is damaged and destroyed by your enemies.

Also I would like you to arrange for your sister to be with my lady of Oxford or with my lady of Bedford or in some other respectable place, wherever you think best, and I will help with her keep; because we are both tired of each other. I will tell you more when I speak with you. I entreat you to do your duty in this if you wish for my comfort and well-being and your honour, for various reasons which you will understand later, etc.

I spoke with the Lord Scales in Norwich and thanked him for the patronage he had shown you and asked him to continue in his patronage of you. And he vowed by his word of honour to do whatever he could for you. And he told me that Yelverton the justice had spoken to him about your affairs, but he did not tell me what was said. But I believe if you asked him to tell you he would. You are indebted to my lord for his good account of you in this district, because he said better of you than I believe you deserve. I understood from him that great rewards had been offered to him by your enemies, against you. Let me know as quickly as you can after the beginning of the legal term how you have got on in all your affairs, because it will seem a very long time to me until I hear some good news.

Also, I entreat you to commend me to the good religious instructor whom you appointed to Caister chapel, and thank him for the great expense he went to on my account in Norwich. And if I were a great lady he would understand that he would prosper on my account, because I believe, from his demeanour, that he is a very virtuous man.

Also, I send you the diamond clasp by the bearer of this letter.

I entreat you do not forget to send me a kerchief of cremil for neckerchiefs for your sister, Anne, because I am put to shame by the good lady she is with because she has none, and I cannot get any anywhere in this town. I would write more to you were it not for lack of time. May God protect you and send you success in all your affairs. Written in haste on Easter Monday.

By your mother.

No. 60: Margaret Paston to John Paston II.[86]

Margaret describes to John II the results of a meeting between Walter Lyhert, Bishop of Norwich, and Agnes and herself, in which Margaret tried to persuade the bishop to annul the secret marriage which had taken place between her daughter Margery and Richard Calle. Unfortunately for Margaret, and despite his obvious sympathy for her position, the bishop judged the marriage vows to be legally binding, and as a consequence Margaret disowned her daughter, who was sent to stay temporarily with Roger Best, a grocer in Norwich. No letters from Margery survive, but a love letter from Richard to Margery dating to this period has been preserved. While Calle continued to work for the Paston family, it seems mother and daughter were never reconciled.

[10 or 11 September 1469]

I greet you warmly and send you God's blessing and mine, letting you know that last Thursday my mother and I were with my lord of Norwich, and asked him to do no more in the business concerning your sister until you and my brother, and others who were your father's executors could be here together; because they had guardianship of her as well as me. And he said openly that he had been asked so often before to question her that he neither could nor would delay it, and ordered me, under threat of excommunication, that she should not be put off, but that she must appear before him the next day. And I said openly that I would neither bring her nor send her. And then he said he would send for her himself, and ordered that she should be free to come when he sent for her. And he said on his word of honour he would be as sorry for her if she had not acted well as he would be if she were a very close relation, both for your mother's sake and mine, and others of her friends. Because he well knew that her behaviour had pierced our hearts painfully.

My mother and I informed him that we could never accept, from what she said, from the words that she had spoken with him [Calle] that either of them were committed to the other, but rather that they were both free to choose. Then he said he would speak to her as best he could before he questioned her, and I was told by several people that he acted as well and openly as if she were a close relation, which would be too long to put into writing now. You will know this in the future, and who were the agents in this; the chancellor was not as guilty in this as I believed he had been.

On Friday the bishop sent for her by Ashfield and others who are very unhappy about her behaviour. And the bishop spoke to her very plainly and

---

86 No address or signature.

reminded her of her birth, who her relatives and friends were, and how she should have more, if she would be ruled and guided by them. And if she would not, what rebuke and shame and loss it would be to her if she would not be guided by them, and the reason for her being abandoned in terms of the material help or comfort she could have had from them. And he said that he had heard it said that she loved such a one as her friends did not want her to marry, and therefore he commanded her to consider very carefully what she did. And he said he wanted to understand whether the words she had said to him constituted matrimony or not. And she repeated what she had said, and said that if those words did not make it sure, she said boldly she would make it surer still before she went from there. Because she said she believed in her conscience she was committed, whatever the words were. These foolish words grieve me and her grandmother as much as all the rest. And the bishop and the chancellor both said that neither I nor any other of her friends would take her in. And then Calle was questioned separately on his own, about whether her words and his coincided, and the time and the place where it supposedly took place. And then the bishop said that he believed that there might be discovered other things in his disfavour that might obstruct it, and therefore he would not be too hasty to give judgement upon it. And he said that he would adjourn until the Wednesday or Thursday after Michaelmas, and so it is delayed. They wanted to get their way quickly, but the bishop said he would not act otherwise than he had said. I was with my mother at her place when she was questioned, and when I heard tell her attitude, I ordered my servants not to admit her into my house. I had given her a warning; she could have paid attention to it earlier if she had been so disposed. And I sent word to one or two others not to admit her if she came. She was brought back to my place to be admitted, and Sir James told those who brought her that I had ordered them all not to admit her. And so my lord of Norwich has left her with Roger Best until the aforementioned day, God knows, very much against his wishes and those of his wife, if they dared to act otherwise. I am sorry that they are burdened with her, but still I am better pleased that she is there in the meantime than anywhere else, because he and his wife are serious and of a suitable disposition, and she will not be allowed to play the fool there.

I entreat you and request you not to take this too sadly, because I know very well that it goes very close to your heart, as it does to mine and to others. But remember, as I do, in losing her we have only lost a wretch, and so take it less to heart. Because if she had been virtuous, whatever she had been, things would not have been as bad as this. Because even if he were to fall down dead at this very hour, she would never be in my heart as she used to be. As for the divorce that you wrote to me about, I understand what you meant but I command you upon my blessing that you do not do or cause anyone else to do anything that would offend God and your conscience. Because if you do, or cause it to be done, God will take revenge for it, and you would put yourself and others in great jeopardy. Because, you can be sure of this, she will bitterly regret her foolishness in the future, and I beg God that she may do so. I entreat you, for my heart's ease, take heart in all things. I trust God shall help, and I entreat God to do so in all our affairs. . . .

No. 61: Margaret Paston to John Paston II.

Margaret expresses her anger at John II because he had allowed the siege of Caister to escalate, with two men reported to be dead, and supplies running low. She urges him to drum up support against their enemies, and states that she would rather Caister were lost than more of its occupants killed.

[12 September 1469]

I greet you warmly, letting you know that your brother and his band of men stand in great danger in Caister, and are lacking in provisions. And Daubeney and Berney are dead, and several others badly hurt, and they are without gunpowder and arrows. And the place has been badly broken down by the guns of the other party, so that unless they have help swiftly, they are likely to lose both their lives and the place, which would be the greatest rebuke to you that any gentleman ever had. Because everyone in this district is very surprised that you allow them to be in such great danger so long without help or any other redress.

The Duke has been more ferverently set on this, and more cruel since Writtle, my lord of Clarence's man, arrived there, than he was before. And he has sent for all his tenants from every place, and other people, to be there at Caister next Thursday, so that there is likely to be the greatest multitude of people that have ever been there. And they intend then to make a major assault, because they have sent for guns to Lynn and other places beside the sea, so that with their great multitude of guns, with other firearms and equipment, no man will dare appear in that place. They will keep them so busy with all their multitude of people that it will not lie in the power of those inside to defend it against them, unless God helps them or they have swift assistance from you. Therefore, if you want my blessing, I order and request you to see that your brother gets help quickly. And if you can find no means, request a letter from my lord of Clarence, if he is in London, or else my lord the Archbishop of York, to the Duke of Norfolk that he will grant those in the place their lives and property. . . . And if you think, as I believe, that the Duke of Norfolk will not agree to this, because he agreed to this before and those in the place would not accept it, then I want the said messenger to bring from the said lord of Clarence, or else my lord Archbishop, to my lord of Oxford, with the said letters, other letters to get them released immediately, even if it means the said Earl of Oxford having the place for the duration of his life for his efforts. Do not fail to get this done quickly, if you want to save their lives and to be esteemed in Norfolk, even if you should lose the best manor of all to secure their release. I would rather you lost the property than their lives. You must get a messenger from the lords or some other notable man to bring these letters.

Do your duty now, and do not make me send you any more messengers about these matters; but send me back with the bearer of this more certain encouragement than you have done with all the others I sent before. . . .

May God protect you. Written the Tuesday before Holy Rood Day in haste. By your mother.

No. 62: Margaret Paston to John Paston II.

After receiving a letter from John II in which he defended the surrender of Caister, Margaret writes to her son justifying her previous letter, and warning him that he is being punished by God.

[22–30 September 1469]

To Sir John Paston in haste.

I greet you warmly, and send you God's blessing and mine, letting you know that it seems to me from the letter you sent me by Robin that you think that I am writing fiction and fantasy. But I do not. I have written as I have been informed, and will continue to do so. I was told that both Daubeney and Berney were dead; but Daubeney, may God absolve his soul, is certainly dead, about which I am very sad, if only it had pleased God that it should have been otherwise.

Remember that you have had two major losses this year, him and Sir Thomas. God chastises you as it pleases him in various ways. He wishes you to know him and serve him better than you have done before now, and then he will show you more grace to do well in all other things. And for love of God, remember this very well, and accept it patiently, and thank God for his chastisement. And if you have been amiss in anything else before now, either due to pride or lavish expenditure or any other thing that might have offended God, put it right and beg Him for His grace and help, and do your best towards God and your neighbours. And although you may have it in your power in future to repay them for their malice, be merciful to them still, and God will show you more grace to realise your wishes in other things. I remind you of these stipulations because of the last letter you sent me. . . .

Also, as for money, I could only get £10 from pledges, and that is spent on your business here, paying off your men who were at Caister and other things, and I do not know where to get any, neither from sureties nor pledges. And as for my own property, I am so poorly paid by it that I fear I shall be forced to borrow for myself or else to break up the household, or both.

As for the surrender of the house at Caister, I believe Writtle has told you about the capitulation by which it was given up. I wish it had happened sooner, and then there would not have been as much harm done as there has been in various ways, because many of our supporters have incurred losses for our sake. And I fear that it will be a long time before it can be recompensed for, and that will cause others to do less for us in future.

I wish you would write to your brother, and anyone else you trust, to attend to your own property, to put it in order and to collect whatever may be had from it quickly, and from John Fastolf's estates peacefully. Because, as for Richard Calle, he will not collect it unless you ask him. And he would like to present his accounts and have your favour, so I am told, and hand over the deeds of Beckham and all the other things that belong to you, because he hopes you will be his good master in future. And he says he will not take a new master until you have refused his service. Remember that your estates can be put in such order that you may know how things stand and what is owed you, because by my faith I have helped as much as I can, and more, while ensuring my own salvation. And therefore take care before it gets worse.

This letter was begun on Friday a week ago, and ended today, the day after Michaelmas Day. May God protect you and give you grace to do as well as I should like you to. And I command you to be careful not to mortgage any land, because if anyone advises that they are not your friends. My advice is to be careful now. I believe your brother will send you news quickly.

No. 63: Margaret Paston to John Paston III.

Margaret writes to John III expressing her annoyance that she has been asked to remove her daughter Anne from the household of Sir William Calthorp. Anne had been placed in the Calthorp household as part of her education, and Margaret now asks her son to help find his sister a husband.

[6 July, probably 1470]

To John Paston the younger may this be delivered in haste.

I greet you warmly and send you God's blessing and mine, letting you know that, since you left, my cousin Calthorp sent me a letter complaining in his letter that because he cannot get paid by his tenants as he has been previously, he intends to reduce the size of his household and to live more economically. Therefore he wishes me to make other arrangements for your sister Anne. He says she is growing tall, and it is time to arrange a marriage for her. I am puzzled about what is causing him to write like this now. Either she has displeased him or else he has caught her out in some wrong-doing. Therefore I beg you to talk to my cousin Clere in London and see what his feelings are concerning her, and send me word, because I shall be obliged to send for her. And with me she will only waste her time, and unless she is willing to be better occupied she will often annoy me and cause me great anxiety. Remember what trouble I had with your sister. Therefore do your share to help her on in a way that will be to your credit and mine.

Also, remember the note that I asked you to get from your brother of what money he has received from me since your father's death. See your uncle Mautby if you can, and send me some news as soon as you can.

May God protect you. Written on the Friday before the Feast of St Thomas of Canterbury in haste.

By your mother.

No. 64: Margaret Paston to John Paston III.[87]

Margaret asks John III to help her to get some money back from his elder brother in order to repay a debt to Elizabeth Clere. She also sends news of the progress of the plague in Norwich, and requests groceries.

[5 November 1471]

I greet you warmly and send you God's blessing and mine, letting you know that my cousin Clere has sent to me for the 100 marks that I borrowed from her for your brother. It chanced that a friend of hers has recently lost more than 300 marks, and he asked her for money and she had none she could come by and therefore she sent to me for the 100 marks. And I do not know what to do about it, because on my word of honour I do not have it nor can contrive to get it even if I were to go to prison because of it. Therefore, consult your brother about it and send me word how he will contrive to get it quickly. Because otherwise I would need to sell all my woods, and that will be a greater loss to him of more that 200 marks if I die. And if I were to sell them now nobody would give me nearly 100 marks as much as they are worth because there are so many wood sales in Norfolk just now. And therefore have him make arrangements about this quickly, if he wants to have my good wishes, and me to save the woods for his greater profit in future times. And send me an answer about this quickly if you wish for my

---

[87]   A draft version of this letter also survives.

health and happiness. Because I shall never have any peace until I know this is resolved. Because she has a bond of £100 for this and it is not kept secret – there are many people who know it now. It seems to me a great rebuke that I gave so generously to your brother that I kept nothing back to pay the debt I owed on his account, and several people who know about it recently have told me so. And when I remember it is like a spear in my heart, considering that he never gave me any assistance in this, nor despite all the money he has received will ever make an effort to do so. If he had only sent me 100 marks previously, I would have believed he had some appreciation of the debt I have put myself in for him. Remind him I have excused him of £20 which the Prior of Bromholm had, which otherwise should have been in that debt. Otherwise it would have been a great rebuke to us not to help him from the money he should have had from your father's bequest. And I also paid money to the sheriff for him. All these he should have helped me with, as well as other things that I have borne over the years that I am saying nothing about. Therefore have him help me now, or else he will suffer three times more, whether I live or die, unless he has more consideration of the debt I stand in. . . .

As for news, my cousin Berney of Witchingham, Veil's wife, London's wife, and Pickard of Tombland have passed to God; may God save their souls. All this household and this parish are safe, blessed be God. We live in fear, but we do not know where to go in order to be safer than we are here. I am sending you 5s with which to buy sugar and dates for me. I should like 3 or 4lb. of sugar. And spend the rest on the dates, and send them to me as quickly as you can. And let me know the price of a pound of pepper, cloves, mace, ginger, cinnamon, almonds, rice, raisins and currants, galingale,[88] saffron, grains and comfits. Send me word the cost of a pound of each of these, and if it is cheaper in London than it is here I will send you money to buy what I want.

Remember I asked you to speak to your brother about the aforementioned 100 marks, when you left here, I believe you have forgotten that you sent me no answer about it. Anyhow, let me have some sort of answer about this quickly, and send me word what success you and your brother are having in your affairs.

And may you both have God's blessing and mine, and may you be granted success in all your affairs in a way that may be to His pleasure and your honour and profit. Written in a hurry on St Leonard's Eve. I warn you, keep this letter confidential and do not lose it, sooner burn it.
By your mother.

---

[88]   An aromatic rootstock of the ginger family.

No. 65: Margaret Paston to John Paston III.

Margaret tells John III of her despair over his brother's inability to repay his debt to her. The issues of John II's expenditure and his failure to have a gravestone made for his father recur in Margaret's letters. This letter may also allude to the influence of Sir James Gloys on Margaret, which her sons believed to be divisive in their relationship with her.

[29 November 1471]

To John Paston, esquire, may this be delivered in haste.

I greet you warmly, and send you God's blessing and mine, letting you know that I have a letter from your brother from which I understand that he cannot, nor will be able to, make any arrangements regarding the 100 marks. This makes me feel very sorrowful, as do the other things which he writes to me about for which he is debt, remembering what we have had before now, and how foolishly it has been spent, with little profit to any of us. And now we are in such circumstances that none of us can help one another without doing what would be too dishonourable for us to do; either to sell wood, or land, or such possessions that we need to have in our houses. As I would swear before God, I do not know what to do about this said money, and about other expenses I have, without dishonour. It is the death of me to think about it. It seems to me from your brother's letter that he thinks I am told by some of those around me to do and say what I have before now, but upon my word he suspects wrongly. I do not need to be told any such thing. I work things out in my own mind, and understand enough, or too much. And when I have revealed my opinion to a certain person whom perhaps he also suspects, they have consoled me more than I could have by any thought in my own mind.

He also writes that he has spent £40 this term. It is a great amount. I think in moderation much of this might have been saved. Your father, God bless his soul, had as much business to do as I believe he has had this term, and did not spent half the money on it in such a short time, and did very well. Out of respect for God, advise him still to be careful with his expenses and management, so that it is not a disgrace to us all. It is shameful, and something much talked about in this district, that your father's gravestone has not been made. For the love of God, let it be remembered and arranged quickly. There has been much more spent wastefully than would have been enough to have had it made. It seems to me that your brother is tired of writing to me, and therefore I will not burden him by writing to him. You can tell him what I write to you. . . .

As for my cask of wine, I would send you money for it, but I dare not put it at risk, there are so many thieves stirring. John Loveday's man was robbed down to his shirt on his way home. I believe if you ask Townsend or Playter or some other good man from this district to lend it to you for me until they come home they will do this much for me, and I shall pay them back again.

Also, James Gresham has been extremely ill and is so still. Juddy tells me that your brother intends to sue him. For God's sake, let no unkindness be shown to him, because that would soon finish him off. Remember how kind and loyal he has been to us, to the best of his ability, and he would not have taken on the responsibilities for which he is in debt had it not been for our sake. He has sold a large part of his land because of it, as I believe you know. Let that be remembered, or else our enemies will rejoice and there will be no honour in that in the long term.

I would write more, but I have no time now. I expect you will come home soon, and therefore I am writing the less. May God protect you and send you success, etc. Written on Friday, Saint Andrew's Eve.
By your mother.

No. 66: Margaret Paston to John Paston III.

Margaret writes to John III seeking reassurances that there is no foundation to the rumours that his brother has been murdered or that he has been attacked.

[7 December, probably 1471]

To John Paston, esquire, may this be delivered.

I greet you warmly and send you God's blessing and mine, asking you to send me word how your brother is. It was said here that he was dead, which caused many other people, and me, to be very sad. I was also told today that you were injured in an attack on you by men in disguise. Therefore, let me know quickly somehow how your brother is, and you too, because I shall not rest easy until I know how you are. And for the love of God you and your brother must be careful how you go, and in what company you eat and drink, and in what place. Because it was said openly here that your brother was poisoned.

And this week someone from Drayton was with me, and told me that several of the tenants said that they did not know what to do if your brother came home. And there was one of the Duke of Suffolk's men nearby who told them not to worry because his journey would be cut short if he went there. Therefore take care of yourself somehow because I think they do not care what they have to do to be avenged, and to frustrate your purpose so that they can have their way with Sir John Fastolf's land. . . . I wish you had never known the land. Remember it was the destruction of your father. Do not place much trust nowadays in the lords' promises that you can be more confident about the support of their men. Because there was a man, a lord's son who said recently, and took it as warning, that Sir Robert Harcourt had the support of the lords after their invasion,[89] and yet a short time afterwards their men killed him in his own home. Little store is set by a man's death nowadays. Therefore beware of deceit, because they will speak very flatteringly to you, who want you to do badly.

May the blessed Trinity protect you. Written in great haste on the first Saturday after St Andrew's Day. Have this letter burnt when you have read it.

Also, I beg you to send me four sugar loaves, each of them of three pounds, and four pounds of dates if they are fresh. I am sending you 10s with the bearer. If you pay more I will pay it back to you when you come home. And do not forget to send me word by the bearer how you are, and remember the letters and record concerning the manor of Gresham that I wrote to your brother about.

By your mother.

No. 67: Margaret Paston to John Paston II.

An indenture dated to July 1470 outlines the agreement between John Paston II and William Wainfleet, Bishop of Winchester over the Fastolf property, in which the Pastons surrendered most of the land, except for Caister. Margaret Paston writes to her eldest son about the sale of lands from the estate and predicts further losses, while lamenting the sacrifices they have been forced to make. She also details the financial arrangements for a marriage settlement of his sister Anne. Anne eventually married William Yelverton III in 1477.

[5 June 1472]

To Sir John Paston, knight, may this be delivered in haste.

I greet you warmly and send you God's blessing and mine, letting you know that I spoke with friends of mine a few days ago who told me I am likely to get involved in a dispute over John Fastolf's goods which were in your father's possession. And as for me, I never had any of them. Therefore I beg you to send me a copy of the indenture for the release from liability that you had from my lord of Winchester, that you told me that you had for both my release from liability and for yours, whatever may be asked of either of us in future.

---

[89]   A reference to the role played by the Earl of Warwick in the temporary restoration of Henry VI in 1470.

Also, I am told that Harry Heydon has bought both Saxthorpe and Titchwell from the said lord, and has taken possession of them. We beat the bushes, and have the loss and the dishonour, and other men get the birds. My lord has bad and foolish advisors who advise him about this. And I am told that Guton is likely to go the same way soon, and as for Hellesdon and Drayton I believe it will remain there as it is. What will become of the rest God knows; I believe it will be just as bad, or worse. We have the loss between us. It ought to be remembered, and those who are guilty ought to have scruples about it. And, so may I prosper, I was told only lately that it is said secretly by those who are at Caister that I am likely to have little good from Mautby,[90] if the Duke of Norfolk still has possession of Caister. And if we lose that we lose the fairest flower of our garland, and therefore help get him out of there quickly, on my advice, whatever happens in future.

Also, it is said here that my lord archbishop is dead. And if it is so, I advise you to call upon his guarantors quickly for money that is owed to us. And out of respect for God, help me to be discharged of the 100 mark debt that you know about, either in that way or some other, because it is too much for me to bear with the other expenses that I have besides that. I am too sorrowful when I think about it.

As for your sister Anne, Master Godfrey and his wife, and W. Grey of Merton have come to an agreement with me and your brother John, if you will agree to it and support her. She shall have as her jointure his mother's property after the death of her and her husband, and I am to pay £10 a year for her and her husband's livelihood until £100 are paid. And if his grandfather's property comes to him in the future he has promised to adjust her jointure. Master Godfrey has promised 40s a year for his part, which leaves it only 4 nobles short of 20 marks a year, which they hope you will make up for your part. William Grey told me he would speak to you about it when he went to London this term.

May God protect you. Written in haste on the Friday following Saint Petronilla's Day.

By your mother.

---

[90] Margaret Paston's parental home.

No. 68: Margaret Paston to John Paston III.

This letter follows another written a few days earlier, in which Margaret had expressed suspicions about Dr Aleyn's wife and intimated that she had feigned sickness in order to avoid an interview. Dr Aleyn had previously sought the help of John III, but in her previous letter Margaret suggested that he might now be looking elsewhere for assistance in his affairs.

[23 November 1472]

To John Paston, esquire, may this be delivered.

I greet you warmly, letting you know that Dr Aleyn's wife has been with me, and asked me to write to you to ask you to support her husband and her in their business. Because she tells me that she is completely relying on you, and if she had been able to walk she would have come to speak with you before you left. Therefore I entreat you to do your duty towards her, because I understand that she is not dissembling, notwithstanding that I suspected her of it, as I wrote to you previously, because she did not come. But I now understand the truth, and that her illness caused her absence here. Therefore I entreat you to help her, because, God help me, I have very much compassion for her and it is very charitable to help her. And I believe she will entirely rely on you and petition you in particular. Also I would like you to ask your brother to favour her, because I imagine that, by the time you have heard her excuse about the business that he is displeased with her husband about, you will consider yourself satisfied.

May God protect you and send you His blessing with mine. Written on the night of the Feast of St Clement, in haste.
By your mother.

No. 69: Margaret Paston probably to James Gloys.[91]

The level of intimacy and trust in this letter suggests that it was sent to the family chaplain, Margaret's chief confidante, and occasional secretary. In it she asks him to accompany Walter, Margaret's fourth and favourite son, up to Oxford.

[18 January, probably 1473]

I commend myself to you, and thank you with all my heart for your letters and for the diligent effort you have made in the business you have written to me about, and in all others, for my profit and honour, and especially at these sessions concerning the business about which I sent you the indenture.

---

[91] No address or signature.

You have lightened my heart by a pound in this, because I was afraid it would not have been done so quickly without liability. And regarding the letters that Thomas Holler's son should have brought me, I have seen neither him nor the letters that he should have brought. Therefore I entreat you with all my heart, if it is no inconvenience to you, that you will take the trouble to take Walter to where he should be, and to arrange for him to be put in good and serious order, because I would be reluctant to lose him. Because I hope to have more joy in him than I have of those who are older. Although it may be more expensive for me to send you with him, I consider myself satisfied, because I know for certain that you will make better arrangements for him, and for the things that he needs, in accordance with my intentions, than anyone else would do. And as for a horse to carry his gear, I think it would be best to acquire one in Cambridge, unless you can get any carriers from there to Oxford more quickly.

And I wonder why I did not get the letters, and whether to lay the blame for it on the father or the son. And I wish Walter to be associated with someone better than Holler's son, where he is going. However, I would not like him to treat him less well, because he is his countryman and neighbour.

And also I entreat you to write a letter in my name to Walter considering you already know my intentions for him. As long as he does well, learns well, and is of good conduct and attitude, he shall not lack anything that I can help with, provided that he needs it. And ask him not to be too hasty to take holy orders that will bind him, until he is 24 years old or more, even if he is advised otherwise; for often haste brings regret. I would rather he were a good secular man, than a foolish priest.

And I am sorry that my cousin Berney is ill, and I beg you to give him my white wine, or any of my medicinal essences, or any other thing of mine in your keeping that may give him comfort. Because I would be very sorry if anything but good should befall him. And for God's sake advise him to get his will made, if it has not been done, and to provide well for his wife, my cousin, or else it would be a pity. And I entreat you to commend me to her, and to my aunt, and to all the gentlemen and gentlewomen there. And as for John Daye, if he is dead I would be sorry, because I do not know how to get hold of the money he owes me.

And I intend that Pecock should have less to do for me another year than he has had, if it can be arranged better with your help, because he has his own interests at heart and not mine. And regarding any merchants for my corn, I can not get any here. Therefore I beg you to do as well in this as you can. Also I am sending you the list of my medicinal recipes by the bearer of this, and if you go away with Walter, I entreat you to come to me as soon as you can after you come home. And I like my dwelling place and the district here very well, and I believe that when summer comes and the fair weather I shall like it better, because I am looked after here almost too well.

And I understand the other business in your letter well enough, for which I thank you. And if Walter does not need to be sent off quickly I would like you to come to me, even if you come one day and go again the next day, then I want to discuss everything with you. And I consider it best, if you do not have the letters that Holler's son should have brought me, for you to send Sim over for them tonight so that I can have them tomorrow, and if you can come yourself I would be even better pleased.

And I remember that mint or milfoil[92] essence would be good for my cousin Berney to drink to make him tolerate food. And if you send to Dame Elizabeth Calthorp, you will not lack one or both. She has other herbal essences to make people tolerate food.

May God protect you. Written on the Monday after the Feast of St Hilary. I have no more time at the moment.

No. 70: Margaret Paston to John Paston II.

At the end of a letter to her eldest son detailing financial problems and concerns about incurring debts to his uncle, William II, Margaret asks him about his health and advises him to return home from London for good. She also tells him that she hopes he will be released from his engagement to Anne Haute, and answers some queries about James Gloys's books. (Gloys died in October 1473.)

[28 January 1475]

To Sir John Paston, knight, may this be delivered in haste. . . . The fourteenth year.

Jesus

Most dearly beloved son, I greet you warmly and send you God's blessing and mine, letting you know that I am surprised that I have had no letter from you since the letter you sent me before the King came to Norwich, in which letter you wrote to me that you would write to me again before you left London. . . .

Thank you for the flasks you sent me. They are very good and please me very well. I shall be as good a housewife for you as I can, and as I would be for myself. Let me know how you are regarding the affliction that you had in your eye and your leg. And if God will not allow you to have health, thank him for that and endure it patiently, and come back home to me, and we shall live together as God will give us grace to do. And as I have said to you before, I wish you were released from Mistress A. H., and then I believe you would do better.

---

[92] Yarrow.

Regarding the books belonging to Sir James that you wanted, the best and finest of all has been claimed, and it is not in his inventory. I shall try to get it for you if I can. The price of all the other books besides that is 20s 6d; I am sending you a list of them. If you approve of their price and you want them, send me word. And also I entreat you to send me an answer to this letter because it seems a long time since I heard from you.

May God protect you. Written at Mautby on the Saturday before the Purification of Our Lady, in the 14th year in the reign of King Edward IV. Your mother.

No. 71: Margaret Paston to John Paston III.

On the same day as the previous letter Margaret writes to her second son in a similar vein, and mentions that William II (with whom Agnes is now living) has his sights set on Oxnead. She also asks him to try to obtain for her, from the Bishop of Norwich, a licence for her chapel at Mautby.

[28 January 1475]

To John Paston, squire, may this be delivered in haste.

Jesus

I greet you warmly and send you God's blessing and mine, letting you know that my cousin Robert Clere was here with me this week and told me that he had not been paid back the money which you know was borrowed from his mother and him. . . .

On my word of honour, I am surprised that I had no letter from your brother before he left London, as he promised in the last letter that he sent me, which was written before the King came to Norwich. I truly expected to have heard from him before now. I would like you to send him word about your uncle's conduct in this business, and to send me an answer about it. Commend me to your grandmother. I wish she were here in Norfolk, as comfortable as ever we saw her, and as little governed by her son as ever she was, and then I believe we would be all be better off because of her. I am told that your uncle has made generous offers to John Bacton and striven to get Oxnead made over to him in law. Whether it is done or not, I do not know yet but I shall find out quickly if I can. I would like you to speak to my lord of Norwich and try to get a licence from him to enable me to receive the sacrament here in the chapel, because it is too far to the church and I am unwell, and the parson is often absent. I would have this granted if possible, because of all sorts of misfortunes that have happened to me and mine. Send me word if you hear any news from your brother, how his illness is, and as much as you know about other matters, as soon as you can. It seems a long time since I heard from him for various reasons.

May God protect you. Written in a hurry at Mautby on the Saturday before Candlemas Day. Send me an answer to this letter soon, and other news etc. By your mother.

My cousin Robert told me that more than £7 of the money he was paid was very rusty and he could not get it changed. He was badly treated in that.

No. 72: Margaret Paston to John Paston II.

Money problems exacerbated by heavy taxation caused Margaret continual worry at this period. Concerned for the safety of her younger sons, she writes to John II, stationed in Calais, requesting him to look after them.

[23 May 1475]

To Sir John Paston may this be delivered in haste.

Most dearly beloved son, I greet you warmly and send you Christ's blessing and mine, wishing to know how you are getting on. I am surprised that I have heard no news from you. . . .

The King is so hard on us in this district, both poor and rich, that I do not know how we shall live unless the world reforms. May God reform it when it is His wish. We can sell neither corn nor cattle for a good price. Malt is only 10d per coomb here, wheat 28d per coomb, oats 10d per coomb. And there is little to be had here at the moment. William Pecock will send you a note of the 2 taxes he has paid for you now, and of what arrangements he has made for the remainder of your corn, and also other things that it is necessary to arrange for in your absence.

Let me know also who you want to act for you in this area, and elsewhere, in your absence, and write to them asking them to act for you, and they will be more willing to act for you. And I will also apply myself on your behalf as best I can. . . .

May God bring you back to this district well, for His pleasure and your honour and profit. Written at Mautby on the 23rd of May, the first Tuesday after Trinity Sunday.

For the love of God, if your brothers go overseas, advise them as you think best for their safety, because some of them are only young soldiers, and hardly know what it means to be a soldier, or to bear up as a soldier should do. May God protect you all and send me good news of you all. And let me know soon how you are, because it seems a long time since I heard from you.

By your mother. . . .

No. 73: Margaret Paston to Dame Elizabeth Brews.

After months of protracted bargaining for the marriage of John III to Margery Brews, negotiations almost broke down. Margaret writes a conciliatory letter to Dame Elizabeth Brews. She suggests that both sets of parents meet at the Brews' residence of Stinton in Sall to discuss ways to redeem the situation. (See also nos. 81, 82, 87 and 88.) The bearer of the letter was Margaret's son-in-law, William Yelverton III (grandson of the Pastons' old adversary, William Yelverton I, and son of William Yelverton II), who had married Anne earlier in the year.

[11 June 1477]

To the very honourable and my very good lady and cousin, Dame Elizabeth Brews.

Most honourable and my chief lady and cousin, with all my heart I commend myself to you. Madam, may it please you to understand that the main reason for my letter to you at this time is this. I am sure you have not forgotten the free discussions we have had on several occasions about the marriage of my cousin Margery, your daughter, and my son, John, about which I have been as glad, and now lately as sorry, as I ever was about any marriage in my life. And where or with whom the blame for the breach lies, I cannot find out for certain. But madam, if is with me or any of mine, I entreat you to appoint a day when my cousin your husband and you expect to be in Norwich, in the direction of Sall, and I will come to you there. And I think before we leave we will find out where the blame lies, and also that, with your and my help and advice together, we will find some way to stop it breaking off. Because if it did it would be no honour to either party, and especially for those who are to blame, considering that it has proceeded so far.

And madam, I entreat you that I may find out for certain by my son Yelverton, the bearer of this, when this meeting will be, if you think it expedient, and the sooner the better to avoid worse. Because, madam, I am certain if it is not concluded in a very short time, that as far as my son is concerned, he intends to do well by my cousin Margery and not so well by himself. And that would be no great pleasure to me, nor I trust, to you, if it happened; which God forbid, whom I entreat to grant you your greatest wishes.

Madam, I entreat you to commend me by this letter to my cousin your husband, and to my cousin Margery, to whom I expected I could have given another name before now. Written at Mautby on St Barnabas's Day. By your Margaret Paston.

No. 74: Margaret Paston to John Paston II.

In her last surviving letter, Margaret writes to her eldest son about a length of gold cloth which she has sent to him to sell to finance the long-overdue completion of his father's tomb at Bromholm Priory, and warns him not to use it for any other purpose. She mediates a complaint from Robert Clere, and encourages John II to pursue his claim to Hellesdon and Drayton in the face of hostility from the Duke of Suffolk. Having heard rumours that John II once again plans to marry, she gives him further advice on the subject.

[27 May 1478]

I greet you warmly and send you God's blessing and mine, letting you know that I have sent you the cloth of gold by Whetley, ordering you not to sell it for any other reason than the completion of your father's tomb, and to send me word in writing. If you sell it for any other purpose, then on my word of honour I shall never trust you as long as I live. Remember, redeeming it cost me 20 marks, and were it not that I will be glad to see it made, I would not part from it. Remember what expenses I have had with you lately, which will cause me hardship for the next two years. When you are better able, I hope you will remember it.

My cousin Clere goes to so much expense at Bromholm as will come to £100 on the lecterns in the choir and in other places, and Heydon likewise. And if nothing should be done for your father it would be to the great discredit of us all, especially to see him lie as he does.

Also I understand that my cousin Robert Clere thinks he has been showed great unkindness in Pecock's dealings with him about certain pasture that you granted to him, and Pecock has let it to someone else he wanted to let it to. Despite this my cousin put his cattle in the pasture and Pecock has seized them. I do not think this treatment is as it should be. I would like each of you to help each other, and live as relatives and friends, for such servants may make trouble between you, which would be discourteous with such near neighbours as you are. He is a man of substance and honour, and will be recognised as such in this county, and I would be reluctant for you to lose the support of those who could help you.

Also, now you have begun your claim to Hellesdon and Drayton, I beg God will send you good luck and success in it. You have as good an opportunity as you could wish, given that your adversary is not in much favour with the King. Also you are reported in this region to be able to do as much with the King as any knight of the court. If it is so, I entreat God to let it continue. And also that you are to marry a close relation of the Queen. What she is, we are not certain. But if it should be that your land comes back due to your marriage, and is settled in peace, out of respect for God do not abandon it, if you can find it in your heart to love her, and if she is such a one by whom you think you can have children. Otherwise, on my word of honour, I would rather that you never married in your life. Also if your business is not effectively resolved now, you and all your friends may regret that you began your claim without taking such a sound measure which might be in your interest, given the many problems that may result from it.

May God grant you much success in all your affairs. Written at Mautby, on the day after the Feast of St Augustine in May, in the 18th year of the reign of King Edward IV.

By your mother.

No. 75. Copy of will.

Margaret's will ensured that the construction of her tomb, unlike that of her husband, would not be neglected by her heirs. Her pride in her father's family is evident from the design in which the Mautby arms take central place. Notably, Margaret includes bequests for John Paston II's illegitimate daughter, and for the children of her estranged and now-deceased daughter, Margery Calle.

[4 February 1482]

In the name of God, amen. I, Margaret Paston, widow, until recently the wife of John Paston, squire, daughter and heir to John Mautby, squire, being of sound spirit and mind, after careful reflection and great deliberation, on the 4th day of February in the year of our Lord 1482, make my last will and testament in the following form.

First, I commit my soul to Almighty God and to Our Lady, His blessed mother, Saint Michael, Saint John the Baptist, and to all saints, and my body to be buried in the aisle of Mautby church in front of the image of Our Lady there, in which aisle rest the bodies of various of my ancestors, whose souls may God absolve.

Also, I bequeath 20s to the high altar of the said Mautby church.

Also, I would like the said aisle in which my body shall be buried to be newly roofed, leaded, and glazed, and the walls of it to be hewn appropriately and skilfully.

Also, I would like my executors to provide a marble stone to be laid on top of my grave within a year of my decease. And upon that stone I would like to have 4 escutcheons[93] set at the 4 corners, of which I would like the first escutcheon to be the arms of my departed husband and myself; the

---

[93] Family shields.

2nd to be the arms of Mautby and Berney of Reedham, departed; the 3rd to be the arms of Mautby and the Lord Loveyn, departed; the 4th to be the arms of Mautby and Sir Roger Beauchamp, departed. And in the middle of the said stone, I would like to have set an escutcheon of the arms of Mautby alone, and under the same these words to be written: 'In God is my trust'; with writing carved in the borders of it, saying these words: 'Here lies Margaret Paston, until recently the wife of John Paston, daughter and heir of John Mautby, squire', and further saying in the same writing the day of the month and the year that I shall die, 'on whose soul may God have mercy'. . . .[94]

Also I bequest 10 marks to Constance, illegitimate daughter of John Paston, knight, when she is 20 years old, to be arranged by my executors.

Also, I bequest £20 to John Calle, son of my daughter Margery, when he reaches the age of 24 years. And if the said John dies before he reaches the stated age, then I would like the specified £20 to be divided equally between William and Richard, sons of the said Margery, when they reach the age of 24 years. And if either of the said William and Richard should die before he reaches the stated age, then I would like the part that should fall to the one who dies to fall to the survivor. And if both the said William and Richard should die before they reach the stated age, then I would like the stated £20 to be dealt with according to the good advice of my executors for me and my friends. . . .[95]

In witness to this, my present testament, I have put my seal.

Made on the aforementioned day and year.

---

[94] A list of detailed instructions for the funeral and the anniversaries of Margaret's death follow, along with a series of bequests to her tenants, to the poor and needy, to various churches and causes, and to religious men and women including anchorites and anchoresses in Norwich. These are then followed by bequests to Margaret's surviving children, grandchildren and daughters-in-law.

[95] Various other bequests to godchildren, servants, etc. follow.

The Letters of Elizabeth Clere

No. 76: Elizabeth Clere to John Paston I.

Elizabeth Clere intervenes on behalf of Elizabeth Paston, in the matter of the marriage negotiations. (See headnote to no. 18.) All of Elizabeth Clere's letters are written in the same hand, which was probably her own.

[29 June, not after 1449]

To my cousin John Paston may this letter be delivered.

Faithful and very dear cousin, I commend myself to you, wishing to hear of your welfare and success in your business, which I entreat God to send you according to his pleasure and to your heart's ease.

Cousin, I let you know that Scrope has been in this region to see my cousin your sister, and he has spoken with my cousin your mother. And she would like him to show you the indentures made between the knight who is married to his daughter and him; whether, if Scrope marries and is granted children, it is the children or his married daughter who will inherit his land.

Cousin, for this reason, pay close attention to his indentures, because he is happy to show them to you or to whoever you will appoint with you. He says to me that he is the last in the tail of his inherited estate, which is worth 350 marks or more, according to Watkin Shipdham, because he has valued his estate many times. And Scrope tells me that if he marries and has an heir, his married daughter will have from his estate 50 marks and no more; and therefore, cousin, I think he would be good for my cousin your sister, unless you can get her someone better. And if you can get someone better, I would advise you to try to achieve it in as short a time as you conveniently can, because she was never so sorrowful as she is nowadays. Because she cannot speak to anyone, whosoever may visit, nor see or speak to my servant, nor the servants of her mother, unless she is deceptive about her intentions. And since Easter she has for the most part been beaten once or twice a week, and sometimes twice in one day, and her head has been broken in two or three places.

For which reason, cousin, she has sent to me by Friar Newton in great secrecy, and entreats me to write to you of her grief, and entreat you to be her good brother, as she relies on you. And she says, if you can ascertain by his title-deeds that his and her children are able to inherit, and she is to have a reasonable jointure, she has heard so much about his birth and social position that, if you want her to, she will marry him, whether her mother wants her to or not, even though she has been told that his appearance is unattractive. Because she says people will hold her in greater esteem if she submits herself to him as she ought to.

Cousin, I have been told that there is a pleasant man in your Inn[96] whose father died recently. If you think that he would be better for her than Scrope, it ought to be canvassed. And give Scrope a kind answer, so that he is not put off until you are sure of someone better. Because he said when he was with me that unless he has a reassuring answer from you he will not pursue this matter any further, because he is unable to see my cousin your sister. And he says he would be able to see her if she were better than she is, and that makes him suspect that her mother is not favourably disposed; and I have informed my cousin your mother of this. For this reason, cousin, remember this matter, because sorrow often causes women to bestow themselves in marriage on someone they should not; and if she were in that situation I know very well that you would regret it.

Cousin, I entreat you to burn this letter, so that neither your servants nor anyone else should see it. Because if my cousin your mother knew that I had sent this letter she would not love me any more.

I write no more to you at this time, but may the Holy Ghost protect you. Written in haste, on St Peter's day, by candlelight.

By your cousin ELIZABETH CLERE.

No. 77: Elizabeth Clere to John Paston I.

Elizabeth Clere seeks John Paston I's advice about a dispute over grazing land in Norwich.

[25 May, probably before 1460]

To my honourable cousin John Paston may this letter be delivered in haste.

Faithful and very dear cousin, I commend myself to you. May it please you to know that there has been purchased from various people of former times a certain pasture and gorse field containing an estimated 100 acres called N, situated in the town of N and belonging to the manor of the same town, except that certain people have 4 acres in various small parts within the same pasture, which are very nearly overgrown with gorse at this time. In spite of this they have, for every half acre, fodder for cattle wandering in the open all summer in the said pasture, paying 4d for the herding of a beast.

---

[96] The Inner Temple.

And in the same pasture I put my beasts to graze and certain beasts that I have allowed to feed for a fee and that do not go into the common pasture of the said town in order to help greatly my tenants. And now they say that it was the custom in former times that the common herdsman of the said town must bring his beasts into the said pasture to graze on Lammas Day. And some people say he must put them to graze there once a month after that day, and some say once a fortnight, and some say once a week, and some say twice or thrice a week, and some say as often as the herdsman likes. So for this reason, after Lammas day, I have to give up my fee and cannot keep my own beasts there unless I am willing to lose them because of lack of food, for the common beasts will overburden the said pasture. And from that time until Candlemas they say they will keep their sheep there.

Therefore I entreat you, cousin, if you agree, that this business can be discussed by learned men, so that I can be sure how I can best conduct myself in this business when you come home. Because I am informed that all together in a body they will begin to guard that common land from next Lammas Day onward.

Also, cousin, my cousin your mother entreats you to remember Horwellbury.

I write no more to you at this time, but may the Holy Ghost protect you. Written in haste on the 25th of May. . . .
By your cousin ELIZABETH C.

No. 78: Elizabeth Clere to John Paston I.

Writing to ask John Paston I's advice about how to deal with a man who had violently claimed ownership of property which she believed she had bought, Elizabeth Clere describes an encounter which took place after church.

[Easter, not after 1460]

To my honourable cousin John Paston may this letter be delivered in haste.

Honourable cousin, I commend myself to you. May it please you to know that Stewartson approached me in church on Easter evening and entreated me to be his good mistress, and wished to submit to me, to do what I ask him to, trusting, he said, that I would the sooner show him clemency because of his submissiveness. Because, he said, if Judas would have asked clemency of God he would have had it, and for the sake of Him whom I had received[97] that day that I would accept his submissiveness. And

---

[97] In Holy Communion.

I informed him that I was charitable, because I wished no physical harm upon him. And I said that if a thief came on the one day and robbed me of what I possess and came and asked me for forgiveness on the other day, would it be reasonable if I were to forgive without compensation? And he said no; and I said that he had applied himself to spread rumours about me and to slander me, for which reason I am more displeased than for any money I have spent, which I did not much care about. And he swore that he had not spread rumours about me. And I said that on another day I should have repeated many more things, but that it is known openly amongst my tenants in this region that when I sent men to his residence to seize goods as payment for his debts to me, he has said, untruthfully, that he was beaten. And on the basis of such untruthful words his master has taken legal action against me and my men. And he swore that he had never said that he was beaten, but that he said he was never so greatly afraid because he did not know what my men would do to him. And I asked him whether or not he would tolerate that my men came into his residence with force and arms, whether or not he was beaten, and he answered with many cunning words. But in the end he admitted that he had said them and that it was said untruthfully, and that he would not say so any more. And I asked my tenants that this should be remembered, because everything that was said was said openly before the greater part of the parish. . . .

Therefore, cousin, I beseech you to send me a letter, by the bearer of this, about what is the best answer to give, protecting my honour.

I write no more to you at this time, but may the Holy Ghost protect you. Written in haste on the Monday nearest Easter Day.

By your cousin ELIZABETH CLERE.

No. 79: Elizabeth Clere to Margaret Paston.

Elizabeth Clere writes to Margaret Paston requesting various legal documents.

[1466, or soon after]

To my honourable cousin Margaret Paston, may this be delivered.

Honourable cousin, I commend myself to you wishing to hear of your health and peace of mind, which I entreat God to send to you. And as for my little cousin, your son is a pretty and happy child, blessed be God.

Cousin, the reason for my writing at this time is for certain legal documents concerning Freethorpe which I handed over to my cousin your husband in order that he could arbitrate between Ramsbury and me, and a paper book of the manorial customary law of Ormesby, and a roll called Doomsday, and other legal documents appertaining to the said manor, and one deed of entail concerning Rainthorpe, which I gave to him, and certain legal documents relating to Claydon and Burgh. And also, cousin, your father-in-law was in the confidence of both my mother and mother-in-law, for which reason I think there might have been left some documents or copies of documents concerning my estates, which is to say Tacolneston, Therston, Rainthorpe, Rusteyns in Wymondham, Keswick, and Stratton. Therefore, cousin, I entreat you with all my heart, when you look through your documents that you would put them to one side for me, as I have complete confidence that you will, because I hear it said that you have properly and conscientiously handed over to certain people the documents belonging to them and I trust truthfully that you will do the same for me.

Cousin, a man from Norwich came to me and found on his way certain rolls and brought them to me, which belong to you and not to me; for this reason I send them to you by the bearer of this letter.

No more to you at this time, but may the Holy Trinity have you in His blessed protection.

By your cousin E. CLERE.

The Letters of Dame Elizabeth Brews

No. 80: Dame Elizabeth Brews to John Paston III.

An early letter from Dame Elizabeth Brews to John Paston III. It concerns a matter involving Elizabeth's cousin Nicholas Derby, which was being arbitrated by Sir Hugh Hastings and Harry Heydon. According to an annotation in the hand of John III, it is also connected with his engagement to Elizabeth's daughter Margery, although there is nothing in the letter itself to indicate this.

[1477[98]]

To my honourable cousin John Paston may this letter be delivered, etc.

Most honourable cousin, I commend myself to you, thanking you with all my heart for the warm welcome you gave me the last time that you were with me in Norwich, etc.

And cousin, as for the business that was entrusted to my uncle Hastings and Harry Heydon, I understand from my uncle that nothing was achieved in it, which I am very sorry about. Cousin, remember what you promised me, that if my uncle and Harry Heydon did not achieve it that you would entrust the business to me. And if it pleases you to do so, in good faith, cousin, I will do as well and as properly and as conscientiously as I can for both parties. And cousin, if it pleases you to come to Topcroft and you fix the day when you will come, I will send for my cousin to be there on the same day. And cousin, I entreat you to send me word back with the bearer of this letter saying what you want to do, etc.

And may Almighty Jesus protect you, etc.

By your cousin DAME ELIZABETH BREWS.

---

[98] Richmond (*Endings*, p.51 n.131) places this letter (Davis, no. 789) and the following one (Davis, no. 790) after no. 82 (Davis, no. 791). His argument is plausible but not incontrovertible. I have therefore followed Davis' ordering.

No. 81: Dame Elizabeth Brews to John Paston III.

Elizabeth Brews writes to encourage the match between John III and her daughter. She also alludes to the business discussed in the previous letter.

[1477]

To my very honourable cousin John Paston, may this letter be delivered etc. Most honourable cousin, I commend myself to you, etc. And I sent my husband a letter about that business which you know about, and he wrote another letter back to me concerning the same business. And he wanted you to go to my mistress your mother and try to get the whole £20 in your control, and then he would be happier to make a marriage agreement with you and will give you £100. And cousin, on the day she is married my father will give her 50 marks. But, if we come to an agreement, I will give you a greater treasure, that is an intelligent gentlewoman, and, even though I say it myself, a good and a virtuous one. Because if I were to take money for her, I would not give her away for £1000. But cousin, I trust you so much that I would think her well bestowed on you even if you were worth much more.

And, cousin, a little while after you left, a man came from my cousin Derby and brought me word that it so happened that he could not come on the appointed day, as I will explain to your more openly when I speak with you, etc. But cousin, if it would please you to come back again on whatever day you fix, I guarantee that they will hold to the same day. Because I would be glad, if my husband and you can agree to this marriage, and it might be my good fortune to conclude this business between my cousins and you, that each of you might love the other in a friendly manner, etc.

And cousin, if this note does not please you, I entreat you that it should be burnt etc. No more to you at this time, but may Almightly Jesus preserve you, etc.

By your cousin DAME ELIZABETH BREWS.

No. 82: Dame Elizabeth Brews to John Paston III.

In attempting to persuade John III to marry her daughter, Elizabeth Brews tells him that Margery has been pleading his cause.

[About 9 February 1477]

To my honourable cousin John Paston may this letter be delivered, etc. Cousin, I commend myself to you, thanking you with all my heart for the warm welcome that you gave me and all my people the last time I was in Norwich. And you promised me that you would never broach the matter with Margery until such time as you and I had agreed. But you have made her such an advocate for you that I can never have rest night nor day because of her entreating and appealing to bring the said business to its accomplishment, etc.

And cousin, on Friday it is Saint Valentine's Day, and every bird chooses itself a mate. And if you would like to come on Thursday night, and arrange matters so that you can stay until Monday, I trust God that you will speak to my husband, and I will pray that we will bring the matter to a conclusion, etc. Because, cousin, it is only a feeble oak that is cut down at the first stroke, because you will be open to reason, I trust to God, may He always keep you in His merciful protection, etc.

By your cousin DAME ELIZABETH BREWS, who with God's grace will be called otherwise.

No. 83: Dame Elizabeth Brews to John Paston III.

A decade after his marriage to her daughter, Elizabeth Brews writes to her son-in-law, requesting his help.

[About 1488]

To my most honourable son Sir John Paston, knight, may this be delivered.

Most honourable son, I commend myself to you and to my lady my daughter your wife, and I send you both Christ's blessing and my own. And, son, I thank you with all my heart on behalf of my son William Brews, and I must entreat you, out of respect for Jesus, that you help him on behalf of your tenants and mine, or else John Dinne will prevail over them.

And, son, may God thank you, you once helped White of Metfield, and so I must now beseech you to act, if it pleases you to give credence to the Prior of the White Friars, because I have told him my intentions. I will consider myself contented with whatever you do.

And, son, we the ladies and gentlewomen of this region who are widows are greatly afflicted by the Bishop of Chester who asks to us to pay more than we are able to; and that is known to Almighty Jesus, who has you in His blessed protection.

By your mother DAME ELIZABETH BREWS.

No. 84: Dame Elizabeth Brews to John Paston III.

Once again, Elizabeth Brews seeks the assistance of John III. This rushed letter may be in her own hand.

[Not before June 1487 or after 1495]

To my most honourable son, Sir John Paston, may this letter be delivered in haste.

Most honourable son, I commend myself to you and to my lady your wife, thanking you with all my heart for the great effort you made on Thursday on my behalf, and for your kindness. Because if another acted as you did, I would have achieved my intention. Therefore I pray to God, do by them as they do by me.

Son, I must entreat you to have a dozen men in harness with bows and weapons appropriate to them, so that I can fetch my distrained goods back. The sheriff's man was with me and one of your men (so he says) and has made me a faithful promise that he will be with me again on Monday. Therefore I entreat you with all my heart, son, and request of you, that your men will be with me on Monday, as my trust is entirely in you, who acknowledge blessed Jesus, who keeps you and yours in His protection.

By your loyal mother DAME ELIZABETH BREWS.

The Letters of Cecily Daune and Constance Reynyforth

No. 85: Cecily Daune to John Paston II.

This letter appears to have been written by John Paston II's mistress in Lincolnshire, who has heard a confused account of a marriage alliance between the Pastons and the Beaufort family. In fact it was John II's uncle, William II, who married Lady Anne Beaufort, daughter of the Duke and Duchess of Somerset. Judging from the request for livery, the uniform given to a retainer, and her stated financial dependence on John II, Cecily may, in effect, have been a prostitute, in which case this document is of some significance in English letter writing history. The signature is autograph.

[3 November, between 1463 and 1468]

To the most honourable sir and, by my faithful heart and service, completely beloved good master, Sir John Paston.

Most honourable sir, and by my faithful heart and service, most completely beloved good master, in my most humble fashion I commend myself to your mastership. May it please you to know that it seems to me a very long time until I will hear true knowledge of your good health, which when it is known to me will be a great comfort to me. And that makes me write to you just now, and also to let you know that I have heard a report that you are going to be married to a daughter of the Duchess of Somerset. Concerning this matter, if I spoke to you, I could tell your mastership something which it would take too long to write now. But I shall and do pray to God every day to send you such a person to be your mate in this world who will respect and faithfully and genuinely love you above all other creatures on this earth. Because that is the most excellent riches in the world, I believe. Because worldly goods are transitory and marriage lasts for the term of one's life, which for some people is a very long time. And therefore sir, without offence, I think marriage should be given careful consideration.

What is more, sir, if it pleases your mastership to understand that winter and cold weather draw near, and I have only a few clothes apart from those you have given me, God bless you. Therefore, sir, if it pleases you, I beseech your good mastership to agree to remember me, your servant, with some livery, such as pleases you, in preparation for this winter, to have a gown made for me to protect me from the cold weather; and that I might have it, and such an answer as you wish to give on these matters, sent to me by the bearer of this letter.

And I will continue to be your petitioner and poor servant, and pray with all my heart to God for your prosperity, whom I beseech to keep you, most honourable sir, and with my faithful heart and service most completely beloved good master, in His blessed care. Written at Hellow on the 3rd of November.

Cecily Daune.

No. 86: Constance Reynyforth to John Paston II.

Constance Reynyforth was the mother of John Paston II's illegitimate daughter, also called Constance. The daughter is remembered in Margaret Paston's will (no. 75). Here Constance makes plans for secretly meeting with her lover.

[21 March 1478]

To Sir John Paston, knight, may this letter be delivered in haste.

Most respected and honourable sir, I commend myself to your mastership, earnestly wishing to hear of your good health and continuing prosperity. And if it pleases you to hear about my poor state, I was in good health at the composition of this simple letter. Regarding the reason for my writing to your mastership: in as much as I arranged to be with you on the day appointed for me, without your good support I cannot easily fulfil my intention unless it pleases you to send one of your men to me, and I shall provide a letter in the name of my uncle, which he shall deliver to my cousin as if he were my uncle's messenger, and by this means I will come at your request. Because my cousin will not want me to leave with him unless it were in the service of my uncle, whose and all others I refuse for yours if my simple service may please you.

And I beseech you to send an answer to this by the bearer of this letter, and I will comply with your intention, by the grace of God, may He protect you at all times. Written at Cobham on the 21st of March.

By your woman and servant CONSTANCE REYNYFORTH.

The Letters of Margery Brews Paston

No. 87: Margery Brews to John Paston III.

This love letter is written in the hand of Thomas Kela, a trusted servant of the Brews family.[99] The initials may be in Margery's own hand. At the time of writing, Margery Brews' father and John Paston II could not come to an agreement over the marriage settlement, and Margery laments her father's lack of generosity.

[February 1477]

To my most dearly beloved Valentine John Paston, squire, may this letter be delivered etc.

Most respected and honourable and my most dearly-beloved Valentine, I commend myself to you with all my heart, desiring to hear of your happiness, which I pray Almighty God to preserve according to His will and your heart's desire. And if it pleases you to hear how I am, I am not in good health in body nor in heart, nor will be until I hear from you. For no one knows what pain it is I suffer and even on pain of death I dare not disclose it.[100]

And my lady my mother has pursued the matter with my father very industriously, but she cannot get any more than you know of, because of which, God knows, I am very sorry.

But if you love me, as I truly believe you do, you will not leave me because of that. Because even if you did not have half the wealth that you do, and I had to undertake the greatest toil that any woman alive should, I would not forsake you. And if you command me to remain faithful wherever I go, I will indeed do everything in my power to love you and no one else ever. Even if my friends say that I am acting wrongly, they will not prevent me from so doing. My heart commands me to love you truly above all

---

[99] For a discussion of the hand of the letter, see the interpretive essay below. Richmond places this letter after the one following on the grounds that the latter 'seems more composed' (*Endings*, p.52 n.134). However, it may well be the case that the two letters simply represent different responses to the same event (one personal, the other more formal), but were written at the same time.

[100] In the original Middle English the main clauses in this sentence and the lines in the penultimate paragraph rhyme but do not scan; the rhyme is lost in the translation. Davis follows Gairdner in setting them out as poetry, although they do not appear as such in the manuscript (London, British Library, MS Add. 43490, f.23).

earthly things for evermore. And however angry they may be, I trust it shall be better in time to come.

No more to you for now, but may the Holy Trinity protect you. And I beg you that you will not let anyone on earth see this letter, except yourself. And this letter was composed at Topcroft with a very heavy heart, etc.

By your own M.B.

No. 88: Margery Brews to John Paston III.

This second Valentine letter from Margery to John III is also in the hand of Thomas Kela.

[February 1477]

To my most dearly beloved cousin John Paston, squire, may this letter be delivered, etc.

Most honourable and dearly beloved Valentine, in my most humble fashion I commend myself to you etc. And I thank you with all my heart for the letter which you sent me by John Beckerton, from which I know for certain that you intend to come to Topcroft shortly, with no other errand or business except to bring to a conclusion the business between my father and you. I would be the happiest one alive if only the business might come to fruition. And you say that, if you come and find the business no further advanced than you did previously, you would no longer want to put my father and my lady my mother to any expense or trouble in that matter for a long time after, which makes my heart very heavy. And if you come and the business comes to nothing, then I will be even sorrier and full of sadness.

And as for myself, I have done and endured in the business as much as I know how to or am able to, as God knows. And I want you to understand clearly that my father refuses to part with any more money than a £100 and 50 marks in this business, which is very far from fulfilling your wishes. For which reason, if you could be content with that amount and my poor person, I would be the happiest maiden on earth. And if you do not consider yourself satisfied with that, or believe that you could get much more money, as I have understood from you before, good, faithful and loving Valentine, do not take the trouble to visit any more on this business. Rather, let it be finished and never spoken of again, on condition that I may be your faithful lover and petitioner for the duration of my life.

No more to you now, but may Almighty Jesus preserve you, in both body and soul, etc.

By your Valentine MARGERY BREWS.

No. 89: Margery Paston to John Paston III.

Four years after their marriage, Margery writes to John III about a conflict which had erupted in the course of an ongoing feud with his uncle William II over Agnes Paston's property (Agnes died in August 1479, having spent her final years living with William II in London). Margery gives advice on how to proceed. Margery signed this letter herself.

[1 November, perhaps 1481]

To my most honourable master John Paston in haste.

Most respected and honourable sir, in my most humble manner I commend myself to you as lowly as I can, etc. May it please you to know that John Howes, Alexander Wharton, John Fille, with the parson and the new miller of Marlingford, have taken the carts of Tom Atwell of East Tuddenham, my uncle William Paston's rent collector; Harry Harby of Melton Magna, my said uncle's rent collector and bailiff; Richard Barker of the said manor of Malton, until recently rent collector of and still indebted to my uncle; and William Smith of Brandon, next to Barnham Broom, until recently rent collector and bailiff of and also indebted to my said uncle. And on last Monday and Tuesday they carried away from Marlingford to the market-place at St Edwards in Norwich twelve of your big planks, of which they made six loads, carrying bows and spears around the said carts for fear of capture.

Sir, as for your tenants at Marlingford, they keep both their livestock and themselves away from the court and do not enter the manor or make any attornment, except for Tom Davy and John Water. This staying away of the tenants is a great injury and loss to them because of the failure to sow their lands with their winter corn. I beg you for God's sake to remember some redress for them.

My Lady Calthorp has been on pilgrimage to Ipswich, and visited my lady of Norfolk on her way home. And there was a great deal of discussion about the business between you and my uncle. He said to my Lady Calthorp that you need not have gone to London, as you would have been able to have reached a resolution at home. He reminded my said Lady Calthorp of the application that he made in relation to the manor of Sporle, promising my lady to observe that and to put it in writing and confirm it as freely as anyone would wish of him. And when he departed from my lady he was not happy; what the reason was I do not know. Lady Calthorp wishes me to write to you to resolve it, because he intends fully to make peace with you. But do not trust him too much, because he is not good.

It seems to my mother-in-law that she has not heard from you for a long time. She is in good health, blessed be God, and all your babies are too. I am surprised that I hear nothing from you, which greatly troubles me. I sent you a letter by the son of Brasier of Norwich, of which I have not heard a word.

No more to you at this time, but may Almighty Jesus have you in His blessed protection. Written in Norwich on the night of All Saints' Day.

By your servant and petitioner MARGERY PASTON.

Sir, I entreat you that it will please you to send for me, if you remain long in London, because it seems to me a long time since I lay in your arms.

No. 90: Margery Paston to John Paston III.

Margery writes another letter to her husband about the same matter. She offers to intercede on her husband's behalf. She also signed this letter herself.

[4 November, perhaps 1481]

To my very honourable master John Paston, esquire, may this letter be delivered in haste, etc.

My own sweetheart, in my most humble manner I commend myself to you, wishing with all my heart to hear of your health and happiness, which I entreat Almighty God to preserve and protect according to His will and your heart's desire. Sir, the reason for my writing to you at this time: last Friday night Alexander Wharton, John House, and John Fille, with two good carts, well supplied with men and horses, came to Marlingford. And there at the manor of Marlingford, and at the mill, they loaded both carts with maslin[101] and wheat, and early on Saturday morning they left Marlingford in the direction of Bungay, or so it is said. The said carts come from Bungay, and I imagine they were sent by Byron, because he has urgently gone over sea, or so it is said, and I imagine he will have the maslin taken over with him, for most of the cartloads were maslin, etc.

Also, sir, last Saturday I spoke with my cousin Gurney, and he said that if I was willing to go to my lady of Norfolk, and entreat her good grace to be your good and gracious lady, she would be so. Because he said that one word of a woman would do more than the words of twenty men, if I could rule my tongue and not speak any ill of my uncle. And if you order me to do so, I believe I will say nothing to displease her ladyship, only what will be of advantage to you. Because it seems to me, from what they and your good steward at Oxnead say, that they will soon reach a resolution. He curses the time that he ever entered the property at Oxnead, because he says that he knows very well that he will make a great loss, and yet he will not

---

[101] Mixed grain.

acknowledge whether or not he has paid. But when he sees his time, he will speak the truth. I understand from my cousin Gurney that my lady is almost weary for her part, and he says my lady will come on pilgrimage to this town, but he does not know whether before or after Christmas. And if I were then to get my Lady Calthorp, my mother-in-law, and my mother and myself, and to come before my lady entreating her to be your good and gracious lady, he believes you will come to a resolution. Because she would gladly be rid of it, without compromising her honour, although she still wants money.

No more to you at this time, but I am troubled that I have received no letter from you. I pray to God to preserve you and send me good tidings from you, and assist you in your business affairs. And as for me, I have found myself a new lodger and companion; the first letter of her name is Mistress Bishop. She commends herself to you by the same token that you would have sent a token to my Master Byron.

At Norwich, the next Sunday after the Feast of All Saints.

By your servant and petitioner MARGERY PASTON.

No. 91: Margery Paston to John Paston III.

Margery sends her husband a note of various domestic and business matters.

[21 January 1486]

To my master John Paston may this be delivered.

Most respected and honourable sir, in my most humble manner I commend myself to you, wishing to hear of your health and happiness, which I entreat God to preserve according to His will and your heart's desire. Sir, I thank you for the venison which you sent me. And your ship has sailed out of the harbour today.

Sir, I send you by my brother William your damask stomacher.[102] As for your velvet tippet,[103] it is not here. Anne says that you put it in your casket in London.

Sir, your children are in good health, blessed be God.

Sir, I entreat you to send me the gold which I spoke to you about, by the next person who comes to Norwich.

Sir, your mast, which remained at Yarmouth has been hired to a ship from Hull for 13s and 4d; and if it gets damaged you will get a new mast in exchange for it.

---

[102] A kind of waistcoat or chest covering.
[103] Scarf or cape.

No more to you at this time, but may Almighty God protect you. Written at Caister Hall on the 21st day of January in the first year of King Harry VII. By your servant MARGERY PASTON.

I pray to God that no ladies overcome you again, so that your business affairs are not delayed any further.

No. 92: Margery Paston to John Paston III.

This letter relates to John Paston III's duties in the service of the Earl of Oxford, in the latter's capacity as Lord High Admiral. It is concerned with a large whale that had been landed on the coast of Norfolk. It also discusses the King's expedition to Brittany. The signature is again autograph.

[10 February 1489]

To my very honourable master, Sir John Paston, knight, may this letter be delivered in haste.

Most respected and honourable sir, in the most humble manner I commend myself to you, wishing to hear of your health and happiness, which may God continue for a long time. Sir, my brother William commends himself to you, and, as for the letter which you sent to him, he had made the meaning of it known to my lord. And it seems to him that it is not part of his duty to have any part of the fish or any money that should arise from it. Never the less, according to your wishes in the letter, my lord has questioned John Atlow about this fish, before John Daniel arrived, about what he had done with it. And he answered, as for the lower jaw of it, he has put it in safety and laid it in a house because your deputy gave possession of it to my lord's use until it might be known whether it belongs to the King or to my lord. And so my lord was very satisfied that it should be so, in so much as the King and my lord have commanded John Atlow that this aforementioned jaw must be brought up to the King in the greatest of haste. Furthermore my brother William understands from your letter that you can make the remainder of the fish worth £4 to my lord. My lord does not want you to trouble yourself anymore therewith because he does not think that it belongs to him. And also, another thing, my brother William has heard it said in the court that the King and my lord will be satisfied should the remainder of the fish be of use to the people of the region, of which you will hear more certainly hereafter.

Also, my brother William said that my lord wants you to send the report of the commission as quickly as you can, and is surprised that you have not sent it up before now.

As regards the breaking up of the parliament, it is very likely that it should not continue any longer, and the reasons are these. My lord the Archbishop of York departed yesterday, and my lord of Northumberland will go on Friday. And also all such people as will go to Brittany will be at Portsmouth a fortnight on Saturday, and the Monday after at the sea board, at which time the King intends to be there to take the musters.[104]

And as for those gentlemen who took shipping to go over to Brittany a fortnight ago, that is to say, Sir Richard Edgecombe the controller, Sir Robert Clifford, Sir John Turberville, and John Motton, sergeant porter, they have arrived again at the English coast, except for Sir Richard Edgecombe who landed in Brittany and was there in a town called Morlaix, which immediately after his arrival was besieged by Frenchmen, and barely escaped with his life. The town has been taken by the Frenchmen, as has the town called Brest, although the castle holds out, so we have heard. And a number of captains have been appointed this season, who are Lord Broke, Sir John Cheney, Sir John of Arundel, Sir John Beauchamp, Sir John Gray, my brother Audley, my uncle Sir Gilbert Debenham, and Thomas Stafford and many other knights and esquires.

And sir, I thank you for the letter which you sent me. Also sir, I have carried out my pilgrimage, thanks be to God. Also sir, we understand that it is enacted that out of every 10 marks of moveable goods, 20d goes to the King, in addition to the tenth part of every person's lands.

And, sir, my brother Heydon will inform you of all other things granted at this parliament, because he has made John Daniel wait all day for his letter, because he was with the King at Westminster and he was unable to attend to the writing of it until night.

Also, sir, Master Calthorp has paid 100 marks to the King.

Also, sir, I have released the £10 to Master Hawes and received the bond from him. Also I have delivered the 20 marks to Edmund Dorman on the orders of my brother Heydon.

No more to you at his time, but may God and the Holy Trinity protect you; and my sister Anne and all the company commend themselves to you. Written in London on the 10th of February.

By your servant MARGERY PASTON.

---

[104] Inspection of the troops.

Interpretive Essay
'In the Absence of a Good Secretary':
The Letters, Lives, and Loves of the Paston
Women Reconsidered

Literacy, Education and Service

Margaret Paston was the most prolific letter writer of the family, followed by, respectively, her sons John II and John III, and her husband John I. Yet paradoxically, she was almost certainly illiterate. She relied entirely on others, whether family members, servants or other associates, to write her letters for her, including her sons, John II, John III, Edmond II; the family bailiff, Richard Calle, and other agents, John Daubeney, John Gresham, John Pamping, John Wykes; the chaplain, James Gloys; and Prior John Mowth.[1] In all, over twenty-nine different scribes wrote down her letters on her behalf.[2] The reliance on scribes, sometimes more than one in a single letter, complicates the idea of a letter as an exchange between two people. Yet we should not deduce from this that Margaret was not in any sense the 'author' of her own letters. In the Middle Ages, composition was an art, whereas writing was regarded as a menial task, and those who could afford to often dictated to scribes whenever possible. Margaret's husband John also asked his sons and servants to write for him and only three of his letters are entirely in his own hand. Alexandra Barratt is of the opinion that

---

[1] *Paston Letters and Papers*, ed. Davis, vol. 1, p.lxxix.

[2] Not all the scribes of Margaret's letters have been identified. Davis argues that one single unidentified scribe was responsible for twenty entire letters and the postscript to another, all written between April 1448 and February 1454. The same scribe also wrote letters for Margaret's husband. Davis' argument that Margaret cannot have written these letters herself is convincing. Given the sheer number of Margaret's letters, it seems equally unlikely that any of the other unidentified hands, found only in occasional letters, is Margaret's. Furthermore, since the subscriptions seem to be in the same hands as the letters, there is no reason to think Margaret could even sign her own name. See *Paston Letters and Papers*, ed. Davis, vol. 1, pp.xxxvii and lxxix; and his earlier articles: 'The Text of Margaret Paston's Letters', *Medium Ævum* 18 (1949), pp.12–28; esp. p.25; and 'A Scribal Problem in the Paston Letters', *English and Germanic Studies* 4 (1951–1952), pp.31–64; esp. pp.41–42 n.12.

many of the female correspondents in the Paston collection 'may just have been too busy, or . . . too grand to write their own letters and preferred to use scribes just as people today might use the services of a typist'.[3] Against this we might note the existence of autograph letters such as a hurriedly written short note in a rather extraordinary large scrawling hand addressed to John III by Elizabeth, Duchess of Suffolk, certainly one of the 'grandest' of the correspondents (Davis, no. 798).[4] However it may simply have been the case that sometimes there was no scribe available. Most critics now think of Margery Kempe as author of her *Book*, even though she relied on others to read and write for her, and even though the interventions of her main scribe, an anonymous cleric, are clearly visible in the final version of her book.[5] In some important respects then, the extent of the Paston women's literacy is incidental. Yet, it may still be useful to rehearse the evidence.

Norman Davis suggested that, like her daughter-in-law, Agnes was unable to write.[6] However this view has been challenged.[7] It is likely that Agnes was actually responsible for one of her own letters, written in a skilful hand that Davis could not identify. Revealingly, the letter ends 'Written at Paston, in haste . . . in the absence of a good secretary' (no. 1; Davis, plate II). If Agnes did write this letter, then she must have written part of a letter for her husband as well (Davis, no. 6). When she came to write her will, Agnes recalled her late husband's concern that he had failed to make sufficient provision for his youngest sons. In one draft of her will, she explains that William I asked her to 'report, record, and bear witness' (no. 16) to the changes he wanted to make. On its own, this does not provide us with clear

---

3   *Women's Writing in Middle English*, ed. Alexandra Barratt (London, Longman, 1992), p.239. For the opposing point of view, see V.M. O'Mara, 'Female Scribal Ability and Scribal Activity in Late Medieval England: the Evidence?', *Leeds Studies in English* 27 (1996), pp.91–92 and 96–99.
4   See Josephine Koster Tarvers, 'In a Woman's Hand? The Question of Medieval Women's Holograph Letters', *Post-Script* 13 (1996), pp.94–95.
5   For the opposite point of view, see J.C. Hirsch, 'Author and Scribe in *The Book of Margery Kempe*', *Medium Ævum* 44 (1975), pp.145–50. For a recent response to and refutation of Hirsch's argument, see Nicholas Watson, 'The Making of *The Book of Margery Kempe*' in *Voices in Dialogue*, ed. Kathryn Kerby-Fulton and Linda Oldson (Notre Dame: Notre Dame University Press, forthcoming).
6   *Paston Letters and Papers*, ed. Davis, vol. 1, p.xxxvii.
7   *Women's Writing*, ed. Barratt, p.239; Diane Watt, ' "No Writing for Writing's Sake": The Language of Service and Household Rhetoric in the Letters of the Paston Women' in *Dear Sister*, ed. Cherewatuk and Wiethaus, p.124; and Laurie Finke, *Women's Writing in English: Medieval England* (London, Longman, 1999), p.190.

evidence of Agnes' literacy, since 'record' could in this context mean oral rather than written testimony.[8] In the context of the other evidence, it supports the argument that Agnes could write.

Of the other Paston women, it is impossible to say whether or not Agnes' daughter Elizabeth herself wrote any part of her two surviving letters. Nevertheless as Davis notes, the evidence of a letter written in Elizabeth's name by her nephew indicates that she was expected to be able at least to add her signature (Davis, no. 388).[9] In contrast, as Josephine Tarvers has convincingly shown, Elizabeth Clere wrote all four of her surviving letters.[10] She also appears to have acted as Agnes' scribe; at any rate Agnes tells John I that Elizabeth has written a letter on her behalf, as he had requested (no. 10).[11] Dame Elizabeth Brews, although she usually relied on others, may well have composed one in her own hand (no. 84).[12] Cecily Daune signed her own letter (no. 85).[13] Circumstances would surely have dictated that Constance Reynyforth's was autograph, were that possible (no. 86).[14] In her one extant letter, Constance suggests to John Paston II that she should either forge or have forged a letter from her uncle in order to facilitate a liaison. Margery Brews Paston is an interesting case. She signed at least three of her letters herself in what Davis characterizes as a 'distinctively halting and uncontrolled hand' (nos. 89, 90 and 92).[15] What is more, her early letters to John III were of a highly personal nature, and she presumably was responsible for composing them, the hardest part of letter writing. Yet although Davis acknowledges that 'she would surely therefore have written [them] herself if she could have' he goes on to assert that 'both were certainly

---

8   *Middle English Dictionary* [hereafter MED] s.v. 'recorden'.
9   *Paston Letters and Papers*, ed. Davis, vol. 1, p.xxxvii.
10   Tarvers, 'In a Woman's Hand?', pp.96–98; but cf. the headnote to Davis, no. 446.
11   Tarvers, 'In a Woman's Hand?', pp.97–98.
12   Tarvers, 'In a Woman's Hand?', p.94; headnote to Davis, no. 820.
13   Headnote to Davis, no. 753.
14   Of the other female correspondents in the collection, Tarvers suggests that a letter written in haste to John I by Margaret's aunt, Elizabeth Mundford, may also be autograph (Davis, no. 657): Tarvers, 'In a Woman's Hand?', pp.95–96. Tarvers does not comment on the letter by Margaret's grandmother, Eleanor Chamber (Davis, no. 426) but there is little evidence either way. Alice Crane does appear to have been able to write, as a letter by Agnes indicates (no. 5), and the one surviving letter from Alice could be autograph (Davis, no. 711). For a list of letters by other women correspondents in the collection that include autograph signatures, see O'Mara, 'Female Scribal Activity', pp.91–92.
15   *Paston Letters and Papers*, vol. 1, ed. Davis, p.xxxvii. Tarvers disagrees with this evaluation and points out that Margery's use of abbreviations in her signature shows her grasp of 'the techonology of writing': 'In a Woman's Hand?', p.93. For no. 90, see Davis, vol. 1, plate XII.

written by a clerk of her father's'.[16] Colin Richmond has, however, recently put forward a counter-claim that Davis' attribution of one of Margery's two Valentine letters (no. 87) to Thomas Kela is incorrect. He believes that Margery wrote this letter, arguing that her hand might well closely resemble Kela's if Kela was responsible for teaching Margery.[17] While I agree with Richmond that the initials at the end are in Margery's own writing, the hand of the main body of the letter is far more confident and practised than that of her later signatures. It is nevertheless fair to say that letter no. 88, which is indisputably in Kela's hand, presents us with a more business-like, pragmatic, and, one might hazard, officially-sanctioned response to the events, setting out clearly the terms of the marriage bargain. It ends rather more moderately with the exhortation that should a satisfactory conclusion not be reached, then 'let it be finished and never spoken of again, on condition that I may be your faithful lover and petitioner for the duration of my life'. In contrast, no. 87, written in rhyming prose (rather than verse, as Davis' editing suggests), is more intimate and revealing. Margery writes about her suffering and love longing, and promises to remain faithful to John III even if her friends disapprove, and entreats him not to allow anyone else 'on earth' to read it.

Whatever we conclude about the extent to which the Paston women could actually write for themselves, we should remember that all the men of the family were evidently skilled in this field, and that the men and women of the family received markedly different schooling. William I had been educated by his father and by his maternal uncle, the latter a successful lawyer. John I went to Cambridge, and to the Inns of Court in London, and his brothers were equally privileged. Agnes took the matter of learning seriously, promising a tutor financial rewards if her son Clement applied himself to his work, encouraging the tutor to discipline him if he did not, and lamenting 'I would rather he were fittingly buried than lost out of negligence' (no. 12). Little is known about the education of Agnes' eldest two grandsons, John II and John III. They would certainly have attended a grammar school where they would have learnt Latin,[18] and been given a more general grounding in skills that might prove useful in the running of an estate or other business. One brother went to Eton. Another, their mother's favourite son Walter, studied at Oxford, with the intention of becoming a priest.

---

[16] *Paston Letters and Papers*, ed. Davis, vol. 1, p.xxxvii.
[17] Colin Richmond, *The Paston Family in the Fifteenth Century: Endings* (Manchester, Manchester University Press, 2000), p.52 and n.135.
[18] Nicholas Orme, *English Schools in the Middle Ages* (London, Methuen, 1973), p.43.

Margaret's comments to James Gloys on this topic reveal that although she did not want to discourage him, she had certain reservations:

As long as he does well, learns well, and is of good conduct and attitude, he shall not lack anything that I can help with, provided that he needs it. And ask him not to be too hasty to take holy orders that will bind him, until he is 24 years old or more, even if he is advised otherwise; for often haste brings regret. I would rather he were a good secular man, than a foolish priest. (no. 69)

Walter, unusually, took his degree, but entering the Church was an exceptional career choice for a Paston son. The legal profession, on the other hand, was financially rewarding, but the benefits of knowing the law were more wide-ranging. Agnes Paston reminded her second son Edmond that only a good grounding in legal matters would serve to defend the family's interests. She recommended that he 'ruminate once a day on your father's advice to learn the law; because he said many times that whosoever would dwell at Paston would need to know how to defend himself' (no. 2). In her view, the courts offered the Pastons at least as much protection as cross-bows and axes.

Previous studies have suggested that, in contrast, the Paston women received very little, if any, formal tutelage.[19] Nicholas Orme provides a rather depressing picture of the education of women in this period. He points out that any teaching of girls, whether in convents (largely the preserve of the children of the aristocracy), or schools, was only provided at an elementary level. Otherwise responsibility for educating girls and young women largely fell to family chaplains. Orme states, 'When all is said, no woman had any strong incentive to do more than learn to read and understand her mother tongue and possibly to read Latin' and he concludes that 'knowledge of Latin grammar or the study of the higher subjects was quite outside her sphere'.[20] Yet Orme also observes that the education of girls and women, even when it did not extend to full literacy and the ability to write, was at least functional:

For women of property, charged with running affairs for an absent husband or left by his death in sole control, [education] gave the power at least to read letters of instruction and reports of servants without which wealth could scarcely be managed successfully.[21]

---

[19] Orme, *English Schools*, pp.52–56; Daniel T. Kline, 'Female Childhoods' in *The Cambridge Companion to Medieval Women's Writing*, ed. Carolyn Dinshaw and David Wallace (Cambridge, Cambridge University Press, 2003), pp.15–16.

[20] Orme, *English Schools*, p.54.

[21] Orme, *English Schools*, pp.53–54.

The letters suggest that this is an understatement. They reveal that it was not only the men of the family who understood the law. William Paston I, as we have seen, entrusted his wife Agnes with ensuring that their youngest sons were provided for. Her competence in financial and legislative matters cannot be questioned. She records that 'immediately after my husband's decease, I opened and declared [the will] to John Paston and all the other of my husband's executors, requesting them to see it carried out' (no. 16). In this context the verb 'declare' has specifically legal connotations of clarification and interpretation.[22] Margaret Paston was not only a canny estate manager, but also a fierce opponent. She played a key role in attempting to defend the manors of Hellesdon and Drayton after the Duke of Suffolk laid claim to the properties. She approached Walter Lyhert, Bishop of Norwich, to reprimand him about the conduct of one of the Duke's agents, who was a parson in his diocese. She records:

I informed him of Master Philip's riotous and evil disposition – asking his lordship to see if a means of correction might be found, given that he was chief justice of the peace, and his ordinary, and given that he was a priest and subject to his correction. (no. 44)

A little while later, after James Gloys and another servant had tried but failed to hold a manorial court at Drayton, Margaret went in person to the shire court. Once again she successfully stated her own case, defending the conduct of herself and her men, and complaining about that of her opponents. She reports that 'when the judge understood the truth, he rebuked the bailiff of Costessey in the strongest terms in front of me and many others' (no. 50). The ease with which women like Margaret use legal terminology and the extent of their knowledge of the processes of the law proves that, either through instruction or experience (learning 'on the job' as it were), women could become extremely proficient in that field.

Education of children was clearly not limited to formal schooling. Aspiring and wealthy families found situations for their children in the households of their social superiors or peers. Children placed in service would learn about social mores, and, it was hoped, find patrons who would be of use to them, and indeed their family, in the future. John Paston II was sent to the Royal Court, but was not very good at putting himself forward. John III, who served the Duke of Norfolk seems to have been more able in this respect. The placements of the daughters of the family were also important, if also not always successful. Having failed to secure a husband, Elizabeth Paston was sent to live with Lady Pole but was evidently unhappy there. Agnes Paston showed limited sympathy to her plight and wrote a reminder

---

[22] MED s.v. 'declaren'.

that she must be told to 'accustom herself to work willingly, as other gentlewomen do' (no. 12). Margaret Paston sought her second son's help in finding a place for Margery in the household of the Duke and Duchess of Norfolk. She told him, 'I would be very glad if she could be offered in marriage or in service in a way that would be to her honour and profit in repaying her friends' (no. 47). When the problem of Margery's involvement with Richard Calle arose, the need to find a situation for her became far more urgent (no. 59). Margaret's other daughter Anne was sent to the household of a relative, Sir William Calthorp, but had to leave suddenly (no. 63). Margaret did not know the reason why, but surmised that 'either she has displeased him or else he has caught her out in some wrongdoing'. Ultimately, however, the main goal of the family, when it came to the daughters of the house, was to find them a husband.

Life in the Medieval Household: Household and Estate Management, Politics and Patronage, Religion, and Health

Popular assumptions about the subordination of women in the Middle Ages are to some extent belied by the evidence of the Paston Letters.[23] Richmond goes so far as to contend that the fifteenth-century was a century of female power and privilege, pointing out that 'in the Paston family it was the womenfolk who were independent and lived in the country'.[24] Anne Haskell takes a more moderate stance, arguing that within the medieval household the wife and husband functioned not autonomously, but as a team, working together towards common goals:

> The men lived in London, maintaining law practices, well connected with legal circles and members of the court. The women lived on the land, overseeing the operation of the estates and maintaining alert and powerful defence against possible challengers. The wife, therefore, was an absolutely essential and obviously equal partner in an enterprise formally consolidated by marriage.[25]

The majority of letters between Agnes and Margaret and their husbands and sons concern matters relating to household and estates. These include

---

[23] For a positive assessment of the situation of women in the Middle Ages, see Eileen Power, *Medieval Women*, ed. M.M. Postan (Cambridge: Cambridge University Press, 1975), esp. pp.35–52.

[24] Richmond, *Endings*, p.74.

[25] Ann S. Haskell, 'The Paston Women on Marriage in Fifteenth-Century England', *Viator* 4 (1973), p.463.

requests for foodstuffs, fabrics and other provisions and for information about London prices. The letters convey instructions about clothing needs, information about land (including the sale of property in the locality), woodland and crops, building work, the trade of produce, and estate maintenance more generally. They discuss rent, and leases and a range of formal and legal matters. For example, Margaret once wrote to her husband asking him what she should do with the malt. She observed, 'if any hot weather comes after it has lain there over the winter season it will be lost unless it is soon sold' warning him that the price had dropped severely (no. 42). The last letter from Margery Brews Paston to John III makes it clear that she aided him in his official duties and responsibilities, keeping him informed about how the carcass of a whale was being disposed of (no. 92). The duties of a housewife were then not only (as we saw in the introduction) at times dangerous, but also arduous and varied. Wife and husband had similar concerns, which went far beyond the upbringing of the children and the overseeing of servants. At the heart of their shared interests were business and profit.

Yet while marriage amongst the middle classes in fifteenth-century England may well have been primarily a partnership, Margaret clearly considered herself to be ultimately answerable to her husband. One letter includes an apology for angering him, 'Upon my word of honour, I do not wish to do or say anything that should make you displeased with me, and if I have done, I am sorry for it, and will make up for it' (no. 33). I have argued elsewhere that the rhetoric of the household that so characterizes the Paston letters acknowledges the possibility of a woman having 'mastery' over her sons.[26] Nevertheless, even if, as widows, the women continued to command considerable respect, their autonomy was limited and their authority often circumscribed. After John II's inheritance of his father's estate, Margaret dominated her eldest son's life. She did not hesitate to criticise him for his lack of prudence. Again and again, she contrasted her husband's care over money with John II's wastefulness. She wrote to John III threatening that if his brother did not repay his debts, 'I would need to sell all my woods, and that will be a greater loss to him of more than 200 marks if I die' (no. 64). She feared the shameful necessity of breaking up the estates and household for financial reasons:

> And now we are in such circumstances that none of us can help
> one another without doing what would be too dishonourable for us
> to do; either to sell wood, or land, or such possessions which we
> need to have in our houses. (no. 65)

---

[26] Watt, ' "No Writing" ', pp.133–34.

In her last surviving letter she implicitly reproached John II because twelve years after his father's death his tomb was not finished:

> Letting you know that I have sent you the cloth of gold by Whetly, ordering you not to sell it for any other reason than the completion of your father's tomb, and to send me word in writing. (no. 74)

She warned him 'If you sell it for any other purpose, then on my word of honour I shall never trust you as long as I live.' Margaret expected her son to be answerable to her, even when it came to the question of how he, as head of the household, ran his affairs, but ultimately she seems to have had only limited control over his behaviour.

If the family household was the domain of the Paston women, the royal court and the households of the aristocracy were largely the preserves of the Paston men. Margaret Paston was present during Margaret of Anjou's visit to Norwich in 1453, but this was an exceptional event (no. 32). Her account is brief, and mainly concerned with recounting a conversation between the Queen and Elizabeth Clere. It ends with the plaintive and very personal lament, 'When the Queen was here . . . I dare not, out of shame, in my beads go in the midst of so many lovely gentlewomen who were here at that time.' In contrast, John II and John III joined the retinue of Edward IV's sister, Margaret of York for her marriage to Charles the Bold, Duke of Burgundy in Bruges in 1468. The second half of the fifteenth century was marked by the Wars of the Roses. Following the brief restoration of Henry VI, John II and John III fought together on the losing Lancastrian side at the battle of Barnet in 1471. Edward IV subsequently pardoned them, and Henry VII knighted John III at the battle of Stoke in 1487. Even if little is recorded in their letters about such momentous historical events, the women were aware that they, and their husbands and sons, were living in dangerous times. In 1445, Agnes Paston asked her son Edmond to keep her informed about the war in France 'for here they are scared to repeat what has been reported' (no. 2). However, the threat was usually closer to home. In a letter of 1462, Margaret evocatively describes the riots, violence and rumours of rebellion of the times (no. 39). She continues:

> [The people] have no love at all for the Duke of Suffolk or his mother. They say that all the traitors and extortionists of this district are maintained by them, and by those they can bribe, with the intention of maintaining still the extortion that was carried out by those who were in authority before. People believe that if the Duke of Suffolk comes there will be a malicious regime unless others come who are better loved here than he is.

Margaret repeatedly feared for her husband and sons, having heard of plots to assault, kidnap or poison them. She warned John III, 'Do not place much trust nowadays in the lords' promises' and went on to tell a cautionary tale about a man who was killed in his bed by the men of his political allies (no. 66).

Alongside practical and economic affairs, the Paston women were informed about, advised on, and even acted in political affairs, at least in so far as they impacted on their own family and working lives. They worked as mediators, trying to bring about reconciliation between the Pastons and their enemies. In one early dispute, Margaret spoke with Lady Morley over the issue of the payment of a fine, but was not received warmly (no. 24). Undeterred by this response, her mother-in-law intervened, 'applied herself. . . very faithfully' and had more success. In the midst of the crisis over Drayton and Hellesdon, Margaret asked her husband whether he wanted her to petition the Duke or dowager Duchess of Suffolk, or indeed the King himself (no. 49). She also recommended he approach the Duke of Norfolk and seek his aid 'because the people love and fear him more than any other lord except the King and my lord of Warwick' (no. 55). Margaret Paston not only kept her husband abreast of who was in and who was out of favour, but also of his own popularity in the locality in times of trouble (see no. 38). When the Duke of Suffolk made his moves on Drayton and Hellesdon, Margaret wrote:

> I have spoken to several of your tenants at Drayton this week, and encouraged them that everything will be well from now on, by the grace of God. And I understand from them that they will be very glad to have their old master back and this is so for all of them except for one or two who are dishonest villains. (no. 43)

Just over three weeks later she reiterated the point, colourfully asserting 'they would almost rather be the Devil's tenants than the Duke's' (no. 46). She also made sure her husband was informed about where his support lay amongst those with political or social clout (see, for example, no. 30).

The Paston women fostered patronage for the family among the nobility. John III believed that if his mother were to attend the Duchess of Norfolk during her confinement, she would serve the family well (Davis, no. 371). In the early 1480s, Margery Brews Paston told her husband that she had heard 'if I was willing to go to my lady of Norfolk, and entreat her good grace to be your good and gracious lady, she would be so' (no. 90). To emphasise her point, she continued 'one word of a woman would do more than the words of twenty men' although she included the qualification, 'if I could rule my tongue'. Of course, this sort of assistance could work in the other direction. In 1467, the widowed and dispossessed Elizabeth Poynings asked her nephew John Paston II to 'canvass the King's Highness' and to use his political influence on her behalf (no. 19).

Turning now to the wider community, we should be aware that in the late fourteenth and fifteenth centuries, East Anglia was a vibrant religious centre of vernacular lay piety in particular, and one in which groups of both orthodox and heterodox believers flourished and expanded.[27] It can be no coincidence that Julian of Norwich and Margery Kempe came from the same part of the country. The evidence of the Lollard heresy trials suggests how religious enthusiasm could be transmuted into heresy.[28] The Paston women, like their husbands and sons, were not fervently religious, but their domestic piety was typical of the time.[29] A major concern of the women would have been to encourage their families in their devotions (see, for example, the postscript to no. 25, in which Margaret urges her husband to attend mass when in London). One of Margaret's earliest letters to her husband, who was at the time ill in London, includes a promise to travel on pilgrimage to St Leonard's Priory in Norwich, and to one of the major pilgrimage destinations in late medieval England, the Marian shrine at Walsingham in Norfolk (no. 22). She tells him that his mother Agnes has vowed to send an 'image of wax, of your weight, to Our Lady of Walsingham' and to pay for the Norwich friars to pray for his recovery. During one of his father's periods of imprisonment in the Fleet, John III wrote to his mother and requested that while in London, she and his sister Margery visit the Holy Cross at the north door of St Paul's Cathedral and the Abbey of St Saviour in Bermondsey. The object of this trip was to offer prayers that Margery should find herself a suitable husband (Davis, no. 323). Near the end of her life, Margaret Paston made another trip to Walsingham (Davis, no. 399). Margery Brews Paston's last letter records that she had recently carried out a pilgrimage, although she does not specify the destination (no. 92). Unlike Margery Kempe, none of the Paston women journeyed abroad, although John Paston III did make the trip to Santiago de Compostella (Davis, nos. 276 and 278). The parish churches were, of course, the centre of local spiritual life, and, as one would expect, the family had a private pew. In the dispute over the building of a wall, Agnes describes how she was challenged after the service, first in the churchyard, and two weeks later in the church itself (nos. 8

[27] See, for example, Gail McMurray Gibson, *The Theater of Devotion: East Anglian Drama and Society in the Late Middle Ages* (Chicago, University of Chicago Press, 1989).

[28] *Heresy Trials in the Diocese of Norwich, 1428–1431*, ed. Norman P. Tanner, Camden Society 4th series 20 (London, Royal Historical Society, 1977); and Norman Tanner, *The Church in Late Medieval Norwich, 1370–1532* (Toronto, Pontifical Institute of Mediaeval Studies, 1984).

[29] David Knowles, 'The Religion of the Pastons', *Downside Review* 42 (1924), pp.143–63.

and 9). Similarly, Elizabeth Clere wrote to John I asking advice about an opponent who approached her in church one Easter, seeking her forgiveness (no. 78). The man pointed out that God would have shown clemency to Judas, had he sought it, but Elizabeth Clere seems to have felt the comparison apposite in other ways and feared further betrayal. Of course the family also had their own chapel and chaplain. As Margaret's health and mobility declined, she also sought a licence for the celebration of mass in the private chapel at her home in Mautby (no. 71).

Richmond puts the case that Margaret was no more than 'conventionally religious'.[30] Yet, even in the face of Margaret's virulent opposition to their wedding, Richard Calle wrote to Margery pointing out that the family would be unlikely to defy God Himself:

> I believe if you soberly tell them the truth, they will not damn their souls for us. If I tell the truth they will not believe me as well as they will do you. And therefore, good lady, out of respect for God, be direct with them and tell the truth. And if they will not in any way agree to it, let it be between God, the Devil, and them. And I pray to God that the danger that we should be in may lie upon them and not upon us. I am unhappy and sorry when I think about their attitude. May God send them grace to direct all things well, as well as I would like. May God be their guide and send them peace and rest, etc. (Davis, no. 861)

Richard was correct: Margaret advised her eldest son not to take any action in the matter 'that would offend God and your conscience' (no. 60). The women's wills are full of conventional piety. Funeral arrangements and bequests, such as those in the will of Elizabeth Poynings, may well be more concerned with outward demonstrations of devotion and the manifestation of social status and wealth than with inner spirituality (no. 20). Nevertheless, Margaret Paston's request that her tomb be inscribed with the verse 'In God is my trust' sounds heartfelt (no. 75).[31]

Recent studies have begun to explore the religious and patronage networks centred on gentry families. Research into patterns of book ownership and exchange has demonstrated that women, whether nuns, anchoresses, widows or wives, had important roles to play in such communities.[32] In East Anglia and Cambridgeshire, scholars such as Osbern Bokenham, John Capgrave, and John Metham, all wrote in the vernacular for women, as did

---

[30] Richmond, *Endings*, p.121.
[31] For an analysis of Margaret's will, see Richmond, *Endings*, pp.122–26.
[32] Mary C. Erler, *Women, Reading, and Piety in Late Medieval England* (Cambridge, Cambridge University Press, 2002).

the Cambridge educated Walter Hilton. The Paston family valued their links with the church. They had close connections with John Brackley, a Greyfriar from Norwich and confessor to Sir John Fastolf, with whom they corresponded frequently. Of course, their reasons for remaining in contact with him were not necessarily spiritual: Brackley supported John I's claim to be Fastolf's main heir. Yet secular concerns did not always underlie the Pastons' interactions with the clergy. In 1469, Margaret mentioned to John III 'the good religious instructor whom you appointed to Caister chapel' (no. 59). Not surprisingly, the most significant religious figure was Sir James Gloys, who not only served as the Paston family chaplain, but also as their business agent and scribe. He was Margaret's particular confidant, as her letter to him dated around 1473 reveals (no. 69). Were the women part of larger cultural communities? Although John II had an impressive library, Margaret seems to have had little interest in literature, devotional or otherwise. Following his death, she asked John II if he wanted to buy Gloys' books, but did not herself express any desire for them (no. 70). Richmond notes that she left no books in her will.[33] Two other of the Paston women are known to have had books in their possession. Agnes borrowed a copy of the devotional work *Stimulus Conscientiae* and her granddaughter Anne owned a copy of the romance *The Siege of Thebes* that she lent to the Earl of Arran (Davis, no. 352).[34] Whatever their levels of literacy, these women were clearly part of some sort of network of exchange. In this context, it is also worth noting that the most overtly religious and didactic letter of the collection, written by Agnes to one of her sons, is also the most literary and rhetorical, and includes, alongside proverbial wisdom, Chaucerian and Biblical references (no. 14).[35]

It is, perhaps, no surprise that religion was considered so important in an era of high mortality. The Black Death broke out in England in 1348–1349 and bubonic plague continued to ravage parts of the country for the next one hundred and thirty years. Agnes, her son Clement I, and her grandsons John II and Walter all died in the year of the last major epidemic. They may not all have been killed by the plague itself, but John II probably was. A couple of weeks before his death, he wrote to his mother from London, telling of his 'fear of sickness' and horror at the unsanitary conditions of his lodgings (Davis, no. 315). References to death and pestilence are

---

[33] Richmond, *Endings*, p.125. However he also notes that at one stage she had two French books in her possession (p.64).

[34] Richmond, *Endings*, p.64.

[35] For a recent analysis, see Roger Dalrymple, 'Reaction, Consolation and Redress in the Letters of the Paston Women' in *Early Modern Women's Letter Writing, 1450–1700*, ed. James Daybell (Basingstoke, Palgrave, 2001), p.21.

found scattered throughout the letters of the Paston women (for example, no. 10). Some of the accounts are particularly vivid, such as this by Agnes:

> And on Tuesday Sir John Heveningham went to his church and heard three masses, and came home again never happier, and said to his wife that he would go into his garden and say a little prayer and then he would dine. And immediately he felt a loss of strength in his leg, and sank down. This was at 9 o'clock, and he was dead before noon. (no. 11)[36]

In a letter of 1465, Margaret explained that Elizabeth Clere had already moved out of Norwich, and Agnes intended to do so, 'because the plague is so rampant' (no. 51). Some years later, Margaret sent news of another outbreak which had killed four friends and bewailed 'We live in fear, but we do not know where to go in order to be safer than we are here' (no. 64).

Increasingly, throughout the Middle Ages and Renaissance, the practice of medicine moved from the female realm into the male; a transition which was of course particularly marked in the case of midwifery. Although Elaine E. Whitaker has argued that 'the Paston women intuitively perceived their displacement as authorities on health maintenance', their letters indicate that they continued to play an important role when it came to healing as well as caring for the sick.[37] Women's responsibilities in healthcare extended from nursing (for example no. 22, in which Margaret tells her sick and absent husband that she would like him to return in order to be able to look after him) to treating ailments (see Davis, no. 389) and even dispensing medicines. Margaret wrote to Gloys:

> And I am sorry that my cousin Berney is ill, and I beg you to give him my white wine, or any of my medicinal essences, or any other thing of mine in your keeping that may give him comfort. . . . And I remember that mint or milfoil essence would be good for my cousin Berney to drink to make him tolerate food. And if you send to Dame Elizabeth Calthorp, you will not lack one or both. She has other herbal essences to make people tolerate food. (no. 69)

It is indeed in those letters relating to the practise of medicine that we have some of the most convincing evidence of female friendships and networks. A particularly striking example is the sole letter from Alice Crane to Margaret, which reveals that Alice had sent her medicine for an illness (Davis, no. 711). Equally fascinating are the letters that refer – or rather allude – to childbearing. Wendy Harding argues that pregnancy was an

---

[36] Cf. Davis, no. 147 for Margaret's account of the same event.
[37] Elaine E. Whitaker, 'Reading the Paston Letters Medically', *English Language Notes* 31 (1993), p.19. For Margaret's warnings against the 'physicians of London', see Davis, no. 177.

'unwritten women's discourse', something that was part of a female oral sphere but which could only be hinted at, rather than addressed directly, in communication with men.[38] Around 1441, Margaret to wrote her husband:

> Elizabeth Peverel has been ill for 15 or 16 weeks with sciatica, but she has sent a message to my mother by Kate that she should come here when God should grant the time, even if she must be wheeled in a barrow. (no. 21)

Harding's commentary is apposite: 'By virtue of her new state, Margaret has joined a circle of women – her mother, Kate (a family servant), and the midwife – who communicate by word of mouth and who are linked through their concern with the maternal body. . . . Only a trace of this unwritten discourse remains in Margaret's letter.'[39] Nevertheless, Harding fails to acknowledge the elements of playful teasing in this and in Margaret's other indirect references to her pregnancy (see also no. 22). Margaret is here surely using veiled allusions and humour to establish a strong sense of intimacy and affection in her correspondence with her husband. Nevertheless, letters such as this do help explain why evidence of female friendships is so elusive in the Paston letters and other medieval texts. Unlike alliances forged by marriage, shared business interests, or patronage, women's friendships were of little social, economic or political import. Only when it comes to sickness or reproduction, and (as we shall see) the arrangement of marriages do female bonds become even partially visible.

Family Ties: Marriage and Love, Children and Friendships

As we saw in the introduction, marriage was crucial to the Paston family's ambitions to rise socially and to extend their landholdings and moveable wealth. A good marriage brought with it prestige, property and money. Alliances for both daughters and sons figure prominently in the letters. As H.S. Bennett notes, 'throughout it is evident that the monetary value of the marriage was all-important; and more, the terms used in speaking of possible marriages are those of business'.[40] This applies equally to the letters of the women as to those of the men. Agnes Paston facilitated the meeting of John I and Margaret, and was pleased to be able to inform her husband that 'no

---

[38] Wendy Harding, 'Medieval Women's Unwritten Discourse on Motherhood: A Reading of Two Fifteenth-Century Texts', *Women's Studies* 21 (1992), pp.197–209.

[39] Harding, 'Medieval Women's Unwritten Discourse', p.200.

[40] H.S. Bennett, *The Pastons and Their England*, 2nd edn. (Cambridge, Cambridge University Press, 1932), p.35.

great negotiation shall be needed between them' (no. 1). She was of course concerned to effect a suitable marriage for her daughter (see, for example, nos. 3 and 4). It is no coincidence that the first of Elizabeth's suitors, Stephen Scrope, was Sir John Fastolf's stepson. Margaret Paston and Elizabeth Clere both got involved in this and subsequent attempts to marry Elizabeth off (see especially nos. 31, 34 and 76), although it seems likely that John I did not always facilitate matters. Following her wedding to Robert Poynings, Elizabeth was concerned that her mother and brother would not pay the money promised to her husband and other debts incurred on her behalf (no. 18). Elizabeth made sure that her will made some provision for her own daughter Mary so that she would be able to find herself a husband (no. 20). Margaret Paston ultimately could not prevail in opposing her daughter Margery's union with Richard Calle (no. 60), but she did succeed in arranging the marriage of Anne to William Yelverton (Davis, no. 352; and see also no. 67 in this volume, in which she outlined a settlement for Anne in earlier negotiations). She warned John II against entangling himself without sufficient thought and care (no. 58) and she must have been relieved when he finally got himself released from his rash engagement (see no. 70). She later advised him against repeating his mistake (no. 74). John III considered a number of possible wives and their viability from a financial point of view. Nevertheless it was Margaret and Dame Elizabeth Brews, who despite Paston concerns that it was not sufficiently lucrative, proved indispensable in brokering the deal which finally facilitated his marriage to Margery (see especially nos. 73, 80–82 and 87–88). Margaret even concerned herself with finding a suitable spouse for one of her female servants (no. 41).

One letter in particular outlines Margaret's idea of what made a good marriage. She told John II:

> If it should be that your land comes back due to your marriage, and settled in peace, out of respect for God do not abandon it, if you can find it in your heart to love her, and if she is such a one by whom you think you can have children. Otherwise, on my word of honour, I would rather you never married in your life. (no. 74)

The priorities are clear: land comes before emotional fulfilment and even legitimate offspring (in other words, heirs). Yet, even if most of the Pastons' marriages were arranged, or at least agreed, by the family, rather than based on individual choice, this did not preclude respect and love between spouses.[41]

---

[41] See Keith Dockray, 'Why Did Fifteenth-Century English Gentry Marry?: The Pastons, Plumptons and Stonors Reconsidered' in *Gentry and Lesser Nobility in Late Medieval Europe*, ed. Michael Jones (Gloucester, Alan Sutton, 1986), pp.61–80; and Richmond, *Endings*, pp.18–58.

The letters of the Paston women combine conventional terms of address with expressions of affection. Margaret Paston wrote thus to her husband during her first pregnancy, 'I entreat you to wear the ring with the image of Saint Margaret that I sent you as a reminder until you come home. You have left me such a reminder that makes me think about you both day and night when I would like to sleep' (no. 21). In her next letter she announced, 'I would rather you were at home . . . than have a new gown, even if it were of scarlet' (no. 22). Years later she wrote to him, 'I shall consider myself half a widow because you are not at home' (no. 36). A matter of months before his death, Margaret visited John I in prison, and then wrote, 'thanking you for the warm welcome you gave me and for the amount you spent on me. You spent more than I wished you to, unless it pleased you to do so' (no. 53). Margery Brews' mother described her as 'an advocate' for her prospective husband John III (no. 82). Margery wrote herself to John III vowing, 'even if you did not have half the wealth that you do, and I had to undertake the greatest toil that any woman alive should, I would not forsake you' (no. 87). A few years after their marriage, she wrote as a postscript, 'Sir, I entreat you that it will please you to send for me, if you remain long in London, because it seems to me a long time since I lay in your arms' (no. 89).

Unfortunately, although unsurprisingly, no letters survive which reveal unmediated the state of mind of those suffering under the pressure to conform to the family's expectations concerning marriage. We mainly have evidence of the thoughts, plans, and anxieties and tensions felt by those who wielded the power. In reports of marriage negotiations, the female parties' opinions and emotions are given less prominence than those of their prospective husbands. Agnes Paston, for example, warned William II when Elizabeth's first prospective groom was losing heart, but mentioned her daughter's feelings only as an afterthought (no. 3). Agnes' claim that she was 'never so favourably disposed to any as she is to him, provided his land is clear as to title' (no. 3) is undermined by Elizabeth Clere's account of the prospective bride's unhappiness (no. 76). When Elizabeth wrote to her mother after her marriage her account of Robert Poynings conveys her dismay at the economic nature of the transaction even as she acknowledges her new husband's generosity:

> And as for my master, my most loved one as you call him, and I should call him now, because I know of no reason to the contrary, and as I trust to Jesus never shall. Because he is very kind to me and is as solicitous as possible to make me certain of my jointure. . . . (no. 18)

In the case of Margery Paston's marriage to Richard Calle, Margaret Paston's anger at the disobedience of her daughter is evident enough. In contrast, Margery's stance is only communicated indirectly through Margaret's repetition of her daughter's stubborn insistence that her marriage was valid: 'And she repeated what she had said, and said that if those words did not make it sure, she said boldly she would make it surer still before she went from there' (no. 60). Nonetheless a sense of Margery's anguish is conveyed in Richard Calle's letter to her: 'I understand, lady, that you have endured as much sorrow on my behalf as any gentlewoman has had in the world' (Davis, no. 861). But of all the letters in the collection, surely the most poignant perspective on marriage is that of Cecily Daune, who wrote to John II when she had heard a rumour that he was to marry. After hinting that the proposed union might be unwise for reasons she did not disclose, she continued:

> But I shall and do pray to God every day to send you such a person to be your mate in this world who will respect and faithfully and genuinely love you above all other creatures on this earth. Because that is the most excellent riches in the world, I believe. Because worldly goods are transitory and marriage lasts for the term of one's life, which for some people is a very long time. And there-fore sir, without offence, I think marriage should be given careful consideration. (no. 85)

This letter may be conventional and sentimental, but it is of a personal nature, written by a woman who believes herself to have been rejected. Furthermore its take on marriage, emphasizing love over money, is remark-able. It is unusual for its time, even when placed alongside the early corres-pondence of Margery Brews.

The evidence of the Paston Letters confirm Alan MacFarlane's thesis that motherhood was not the 'central, only and defining role of women'.[42] Yet although the women of the family engaged in a wide range of other activ-ities, they shared with their husbands a series of responsibilities towards their children: they had them educated, placed them in service, and tried to arrange suitable marriages. Bringing up sons in particular could prove a costly business, but it was also an investment, financial and emotional. Relations between mothers and sons, especially the eldest sons and heirs, are, as might be expected given the extent to which the women worked for them and their interests, well documented in the letters. At the time of her husband's death, Agnes Paston fell out with John I. The different drafts of her will describe how she was defied by her son, whom she represents as self-seeking and little more than a thief (nos. 15–17). Agnes explained that some of the family property should go to William II and Clement. John I did

---

[42] Alan MacFarlane, *Marriage and Love in England: Modes of Reproduction 1300–1840* (Oxford, Blackwell, 1986), p.61.

not agree and, Agnes states, 'after that [he] never had any very kind words to say to me' (no. 17).[43] There are no letters from Agnes to John I between 1453 and 1461. In a letter dated some eight years after William I's death, Agnes urged John I 'apply yourself so that something can be purchased for your two brothers' (no. 10). Nevertheless, she was willing to pardon him when asked to, as a letter of 1465 reveals:

> Son, I greet you warmly and let you know that since your brother Clement tells me that you sincerely desire my blessing, may that blessing that I begged your father to give you the last day ever that he spoke and the blessing of all saints under heaven and mine come to you all days and times. And truthfully only believe that you have it, and you shall have it, provided that I find you kind and minded towards the well-being of your father's soul and for the welfare of your brothers. (no. 14)

But while Agnes may have felt that the responsibility had fallen to her to look after her youngest sons, since her eldest was not willing to, she was not a gentle mother (see especially, no. 12) and it is difficult to assess how close they were to her. Agnes' last years were spent with William II in London. Shortly after Agnes had moved there, Margaret wrote to John III, 'Commend me to your grandmother. I wish she were here in Norfolk, as comfortable as ever we saw her, and as little governed by her son as ever she was, and then I believe we would all be better off because of her' (no. 71). The final clause is revealing. Margaret suspected that William II's decision to care for his mother in her old age was motivated less by kindness and a sense of filial duty than by greed (his hope to benefit from her will). At the same time, she betrays her own self-interest and concern for her children's benefit.

Margaret Paston played the important role of intermediary between Agnes, for whom she seems to have had a genuine affection, and her husband (see, for example, no. 44), and also between her husband and their eldest son. It is MacFarlane's opinion that in the medieval and early modern periods, children sometimes had little sense of responsibility towards their mother and father,[44] but the evidence of the Paston letters goes against this. Parents expected their children to be attentive, polite, considerate, and obedient.[45]

---

[43] On the dispute over the will, see Colin Richmond, *The Paston Family in the Fifteenth Century: the First Phase* (Cambridge, Cambridge University Press, 1990), pp.167–205; and Joel T. Rosenthal, 'Looking for Grandmother: the Pastons and their Counterparts in Late Medieval England' in *Medieval Mothering*, ed. John Carmi Parsons and Bonnie Wheeler (New York, Garland, 1996), p.265.

[44] MacFarlane, *Marriage and Love*, p.108.

[45] Nicholas Orme, *Medieval Children* (New Haven, Yale University Press, 2003), p.84.

In a series of letters from the mid–1460s, Margaret wrote first to John II himself, expressing her own displeasure at his actions, and urging John II to reform (no. 41). Well over a year later, she asked her husband to forgive him (no. 42), and, when he was finally due to be readmitted into the family home, she promised not to condone 'any low behaviour' (no. 43). After his father's death, John II earned his mother's displeasure by dishonestly dealing with financial matters, and in other affairs involving the running of the estate, including selling land, and in the recurring issue of his neglect in having his father's gravestone made. Margaret frequently wrote to John III complaining about his brother's carelessness with money (for example, no. 65). John III himself was not exempt from maternal exhortation. Margaret once reminded him to 'avoid such things I spoke to you about last time in our parish church' and entreated God to make him 'as virtuous a man as any of your kin has ever been' (no. 47).

When John I died, it seems that it was not in fact John II who replaced his father in Margaret's affections, but the chaplain, Gloys,[46] and her sons' letters reveal their jealousy and displeasure. John Paston III for one felt that his own and his brother Edmund's place in his mother's favour had been usurped. He described the scene at home vividly:

> Quarrels are always being picked to get my brother E. [Edmund] and me out of her house. It is not easy to avoid being chastised by the time we go to bed. All that we do we do badly, and all that Sir James and Pecock do is done well. Sir James and I are at odds. We fell out before my mother with 'Thou proud priest' and 'Thou proud squire', my mother taking his part, so I have almost shat the boat[47] at my mother's house. . . . My mother proposes in haste to make an account of all her lands and upon that account to make her will. . . . And in this anger between Sir James and me she has promised me that my part shall be nought; what yours shall be I cannot say. (Davis, no. 353)

In his next letter on the subject, he complains that Gloys is always 'chopping' at him in front of his mother, but that he responds by smiling and telling Gloys that 'it is good hearing these old tales' (Davis, no. 355).[48] Margaret may have been disappointed in most of her children, but she told Gloys that she had greater hopes of Walter, whom she entrusted to his care: 'I would be reluctant to lose him. Because I hope to have more joy of him than I have

---

[46] See Richmond, *Endings*, pp.113–15; Richmond points out that 'between John I's death in 1466 and his own in 1473 Gloys wrote for Margaret thirteen and a half of her twenty-one letters' (p.114).

[47] 'Made myself unwelcome'.

[48] Cf. also no. 65 in this volume.

of those who are older' (no. 69). At the same time, Margaret was concerned about the safety and welfare of all her sons (for example nos. 66 and 72). Like Agnes, Margaret wanted John II to look after his brothers and she was extremely angry when she thought he had risked the lives of John III and two of his men at the siege of Caister (nos. 61 and 62). She ascribed his bad luck to divine chastisement and blamed his losses on his sinfulness, either 'pride or lavish expenditure or any other thing that might have offended God' (no. 62). Once, when he was ill in London, she was more sympathetic, but she advised him to be stoical, 'if God will not allow you to have health, thank him for that and endure it patiently' (no. 70).

While relations between mothers and sons were not always easy, those between mothers and daughters were far worse. The Paston women must have spent much, if not most, of their time in the company of other women, especially their mothers and daughters. The women must have lived, worked and socialised together. They would therefore have less reason to write to one another. On the rare occasions when they did correspond, their letters, as might be expected, are largely concerned with business matters. Thus Margaret Paston wrote to Dame Elizabeth Brews to arrange a meeting to try to sort out the business of the marriage of their children (no. 73). Likewise, Elizabeth Clere wrote to Margaret to request the return of some important deeds and documents relating to her property (no. 79). The one exception to this rule is a letter from Alice Crane to Margaret Paston (Davis, no. 711). Alice enquires about Margaret's health and apologizes for not having written sooner, expressing her gratitude for 'the great friendship' shown to her mother and for 'the great welcome that I had from you when I was with you last'. Nevertheless, even here Alice asks Margaret to seek John II's assistance in a matter relating to her father. It may have been that some of the women's letters were not preserved. Of the two surviving letters written by Agnes' daughter Elizabeth, one, to Agnes herself, relates to her first marriage (no. 18), the other, to her eldest brother, to the fact that after Robert Poynings died she found herself dispossessed of her property (no. 19).

Mothers played an important role in the education of their daughters,[49] as well as in the mediation of their marriages. Despite this, the letters reveal considerable hostility between women of different generations. Haskell talks about 'the intractable attitudes of medieval mothers toward their daughters'[50] and Nancy Stiller describes the 'cruel attempts at subjugating [one's] daughter'.[51] At the time when Scrope was being proposed as a

[49] Orme, *English Schools*, pp. 52–56.
[50] Haskell, 'Paston Women on Marriage', p.469.
[51] Nancy Stiller, *Eve's Orphans: Mothers and Daughters in Medieval English Literature* (Westport, Connecticut, Greenwood Press, 1980), p.50.

husband for Elizabeth Paston, Elizabeth Clere wrote to John I urging him
to find another suitor as quickly as possible:

> Because she [Elizabeth] cannot speak to anyone, whosoever may
> visit, nor see or speak to my servant, nor the servants of her mother,
> unless she is deceptive about her intentions. And since Easter she
> has for the most part been beaten once or twice a week, and some-
> times twice in one day, and her head has been broken in two or
> three places.
>
> For which reason, cousin, she has sent to me by Friar Newton in
> great secrecy, and entreats me to write to you of her grief, and
> entreat you to be her good brother, as she relies on you. (no. 76)

When these and subsequent arrangements fell through, Agnes was des-
perate to have Elizabeth out of the house. Margaret told her husband that 'It
seems from my mother's [Agnes'] words that she would never be so glad
to be free of her as she is now' (no. 34). Margaret Paston was likewise keen
to find situations for her daughters to free her of their company. She told her
eldest son that it was imperative to find a place for Margery 'because we
are both tired of each other' (no. 59). Likewise, in a letter to John Paston III,
Margaret tells him that his sister Anne 'is growing tall' and it is high
time to find her a husband. She continues, 'I shall be obliged to send for
her. And with me she will only waste her time, and unless she is willing to
be better occupied she will often annoy me and cause me great anxiety.
Remember what trouble I had with your sister' (no. 63). For the most part,
we can only surmise the nature of the daughter's feelings towards their
mothers. The one letter we have to Agnes Paston from the newly-married
Elizabeth Poynings reveals a humble, almost chilling formality in its opening lines:

> Very honourable and my most dearly beloved mother, in the most
> humble fashion I commend myself to your good motherhood,
> beseeching you daily and nightly for your motherly blessing,
> wishing ever more to hear of your good health and prosperity,
> which I pray to God to continue and increase according to your
> heart's desire. And if it pleased your good motherhood to hear of
> me, and how I do, at the time that this letter was composed I was
> in good bodily health, thanks be to Jesus. (no. 18)

The conventionality of the extended greeting contrasts with the
reproachful tone of the body of the letter. It may be possible to detect here
an underlying rebelliousness on the part of Elizabeth against the subjection
under which she found herself.

What then is the cause of such ill feeling between mothers and daughters? Haskell suggests that sons were more important, not only as heirs and
money earners, but also for psychological reasons. It was believed that 'strong

men produced sons', and consequently 'the women who produced [daughters] lived with a double anguish, originally for having disappointed their fathers, and subsequently for having been the instruments of revealing their husbands' weakness'.[52] There is certainly no suggestion in the letters of the Paston men that the fathers showed any particular interest in their daughters, let alone any affection. Stiller suggests that in assuming an authoritarian attitude, women adopted the role of a substitute father. Developing Haskell's argument that many medieval women may have felt deep resentment towards their daughters because they both identified with and despised their vulnerability, she suggests that it would have been virtually impossible for women to love or nurture one another. To survive a daughter would in turn have to re-identify herself with her 'active masculine mother' and consequently the formation of deep emotional relationships with other women became increasingly unlikely.[53] It is difficult to contradict this view. The only mother to overtly praise her daughter was Dame Elizabeth Brews, who wrote to John III, 'if we come to an agreement, I will give you a greater treasure, that is an intelligent gentlewomen, and, even though I say it myself, a good and a virtuous one' (no. 81). In this case, however, Elizabeth Brews is engaged in what amounts to a financial transaction, as she herself acknowledges: 'Because if I were to take money for her, I would not give her away for £1000.' She wants to convince John III that even if the money is not right, he is still getting a bargain. On the other hand, Margaret Paston did seem to be genuinely upset by what she perceived as her daughter's betrayal, and believed her eldest son would share her grief:

> I entreat you and request you not to take this too sadly, because I know very well that it goes very close to your heart, as it does to mine and to others. But remember, as I do, in losing her we have only lost a wretch, and so take it less to heart. Because if she had been virtuous, whatever she had been, things would not have been as bad as this. Because even if he [Richard Calle] were to fall down dead at this very hour, she would never be in my heart as she used to be. (no. 60)

---

[52] Haskell, 'Paston Women on Marriage', pp.469–70. We might be reminded of Hildegard of Bingen's argument that the degree of affection felt between a man and a woman at the time of conception combined with the 'strength' of the man's semen were key factors in determining the child's gender and disposition. Unreciprocated love and weak semen resulted in the birth of a female child of bitter disposition. See Hildegard of Bingen, *On Natural Philosophy and Medicine: Selections from Cause et Cure*, trans. Margret Berger (Cambridge, D.S. Brewer, 1999), pp.51–52. For the wider scientific context, see Joan Cadden, *Meanings of Sex Difference in the Middle Ages: Medicine, Science, and Culture* (Cambridge, Cambridge University Press, 1993), pp.130–34.

[53] Stiller, *Eve's Orphans*, pp.51–52.

At the same time as she cursed and ostracised her daughter, Margaret betrayed the depths of her attachment to her.

Although mothers did not routinely exchange letters with their daughters and we have no letters between sisters and very little in the way of informal correspondence between women, it is still possible to see evidence of women's friendship.[54] Agnes and Margaret presented a united front on a number of issues relating to the family. Agnes, for example, seems to have been the first to suggest that Margaret and John I should start to look for a husband for their eldest daughter (no. 40). Margaret did not disagree. Likewise, Agnes supported Margaret before the Bishop of Norwich when they tried to get Margery's betrothal to Richard Calle rendered invalid (no. 60). Nevertheless, Margaret Paston also wrote to her husband encouraging him to help his sister Elizabeth in the search for a husband, pointing out that Agnes 'speaks to her [Elizabeth] in a way that she thinks is very unfriendly, and she is very tired of it' (no. 31). In the same letter she reminded him of a promise to help Alice Crane in 'her business', adding that her friend was losing sleep with worry.[55] Margaret also had to rebuild bridges between Elizabeth Clere and John I following a distancing between them (no. 51). We can also see from the wills of Elizabeth Paston Browne and Margaret Paston that they did value female relatives, extended family and friends, and servants.[56] Elizabeth not only provided for her daughter, but stated that in the event of her death the bequest should go to a kinswoman called Margaret Hasslake, and, in the event of her death, to her daughter-in-law Dame Isabel Poynings (no. 20). She did not, however, leave anything to any of the Pastons, of either sex. Margaret Paston seems to have found her daughter-in-law Margery to be reliable. She entrusted her with the responsibility of ensuring her wishes were fulfilled after her death (Davis, no. 386). Margaret did not include Elizabeth Clere in her will, but she did leave a bequest for John II's illegitimate child Constance and mention her dead daughter Margery's sons (no. 75). However, one document more than any other in the collection reveals that strong ties between women did exist. When Elizabeth Clere wrote to her cousin John I expressing the hope that he would alleviate his sister's suffering under her mother's wrath, she realised

---

54 The key study of this topic is Colin Richmond, 'Elizabeth Clere: Friend of the Pastons' in *Medieval Women: Texts and Contexts in Late Medieval Britain, Essays for Felicity Riddy*, ed. Jocelyn Wogan-Browne, Rosalynn Voaden, Arlyn Diamond, Ann Hutchison, Carol. M. Meale and Lesley Johnson (Turnhout, Brepols. 2000), pp.251–73.

55 Cf. no. 5 for Agnes seeking help on behalf of Alice Crane.

56 Compare Elizabeth Clere's will: Richmond, 'Elizabeth Clere', pp.265–72. Richmond notes Elizabeth's generosity to her granddaughters and to other women.

that if Agnes discovered the letter 'she would not love me any more' and asked for it to be destroyed on receipt (no. 76). It is a testimony to her sisterly feelings she was nevertheless willing to run the risk on behalf of the long-suffering Elizabeth. She emphasised that under the pressure of Agnes' cruel treatment Elizabeth was on the point of giving in 'even though she has been told that [Scrope's] appearance is unattractive' and warned John I that 'sorrow often causes women to bestow themselves in marriage on someone they should not'. Although Elizabeth Clere did not lose sight of the financial aspect of the situation – she did not advise putting Scrope off before a better suitor was found – this is a striking, if somewhat isolated, example of the deep compassion felt by one women for another.

In conclusion, the letters of the Paston women reveal that they usually had a good working knowledge of the law and of matters relating to the running of an estate, even if they lacked a formal education, were not fully literate, and had only limited interest in books and reading. The women played a major role in the running of the household and the estates, were informed about issues of politics and patronage, and took responsibility for the piety of the family and health matters. Even if marriages were usually contracted primarily for financial reasons, the women's relationships with men, as husbands and sons, were central to their lives and dominate the letters. Daughters are often discussed only when they prove difficult and disobedient, but female friendship could be as enduring as marriage, and the women evidently valued such ties. By listening solely to the women correspondents, rather than to a cacophony of male and female voices, we can learn more about the women's lives, about their hopes and anxieties, and about their bonds to one another. Finally, we should not overlook the fact that writing – *letter* writing – was an important activity for these women, and it was one that would be undertaken in all sorts of unfavourable circumstances, and even, as Agnes puts it, in the absence of a good secretary.

Suggestions for Further Reading

A great deal has been published on the subject of the Paston family in the fifteenth century in recent decades. Many of these books and articles make only passing reference to the women. Here I have restricted myself to the major editions of the letters and papers, and to publications of general literary and historical interest that are of immediate relevance either to the Paston women or to medieval and early modern letters generally.

Editions and Translations

Barber, Richard, ed., *The Pastons: A Family in the Wars of the Roses* (Woodbridge, The Boydell Press, 1993).
  A good selection of letters in modern spelling, with contextual material.
Davis, Norman, ed., *Paston Letters and Papers of the Fifteenth Century*, 2 vols. (Oxford, Clarendon Press, 1971 and 1976).
  The standard edition. Volume 1 is available online in machine-readable format, prepared for the University of Virginia Electronic Text Center in 1993.
——, ed.; *The Paston Letters: A Selection in Modern Spelling* (Oxford, Oxford University Press, 1983).
  A useful sample of the letters.
Gairdner, John, ed., *The Paston Letters, A.D. 1422–1509*, 6 vols. (London, Chatto and Windus, 1904).
  An incomplete edition, with some errors in dating and attribution.
Virgoe, Roger, ed., *Private Life in the Fifteenth Century: Illustrated Letters of the Paston Family* (London, Macmillan, 1989).
  A full-colour illustrated edition of selected letters in translation with useful contextual material. For the general reader.
Warrington, John, ed., *The Paston Letters*, 2 vols. (London, Dent, 1956).
  A revised text of a translation first published in 1924. Based on Gairdner's edition.

Secondary Reading

Bennett, H.S., *The Pastons and Their England*, 2nd edn. (Cambridge, Cambridge University Press, 1932).

A dated but still useful historical account of the Pastons in the fifteenth century. Includes key chapters on marriage, love, women's life, parents and children, houses and furniture, education and books, letters and letter-writing, and religion.

Bosse, Roberta Bux, 'Female Sexual Behavior in the Late Middle Ages: Ideal and Actual', *Fifteenth-Century Studies* 10 (1984), pp.15–37.

An article looking at attitudes to female sexuality in Holy Maidenhood, The Book of the Knight of La Tour Landry, the letters of Margaret Paston, and The Book of Margery Kempe.

Cherewatuk, Karen and Ulrike Wiethaus, eds., *Dear Sister: Medieval Women and the Epistolary Genre* (Philadelphia, University of Pennsylvania Press, 1993), pp.122–38.

A ground-breaking study with chapters on Radegund, Hildegard of Bingen, Héloïse, Catherine of Siena, the Paston women, Christine de Pizan and Maria de Hout. Helpful introduction.

Classen, Albrecht, 'Female Epistolary Literature from Antiquity to the Present: An Introduction', *Studia Neophilologia* 60 (1988), pp.3–13.

A good survey of women's letters in Europe from the Roman and Carolingian periods to the twentieth century.

Constable, Giles, *Letters and Letter-Collections* (Turnhout, Brepols, 1976).

A broad survey discussing letters as a genre, editions of letters, and their historical value. Also addresses important questions of production, composition (including authorship and style), transmission and preservation.

Dalrymple, Roger, 'Reaction, Consolation and Redress in the Letters of the Paston Women' in *Early Modern Women's Letter Writing, 1450–1700*, ed. James Daybell (Basingstoke, Palgrave, 2001), pp.16–28.

A chapter concentrating on the letters of Agnes and Margaret Paston. Argues that in addition to serving practical concerns, they are written to convey news, offer consolation, or correct false report.

Davis, Norman, 'That Language of the Pastons', *Proceedings of the British Academy* 40 (1955), pp.119–44.

A study of language and style.

——, 'The *Litera Troili* and English Letters', *Review of English Studies*, n.s. 16 (1965), pp.233–44.

A study examining the Paston letters in the light of epistolary conventions.

——, 'Style and Stereotype in Early English Letters', *Leeds Studies in English*, n.s. 1 (1967), pp.7–17.

A study looking at the stylistic range of the Paston letters, from the proverbial to the literary.

Daybell, James, ed., *Early Modern Women's Letter Writing, 1450–1700* (Basingstoke, Palgrave, 2001).

An excellent collection of essays with a very useful introduction, which considers both how women's letters should be analysed and what they can reveal.

Dockray, Keith, 'Why Did Fifteenth-Century English Gentry Marry?: The Pastons, Plumptons and Stonors Reconsidered' in *Gentry and Lesser Nobility in Late Medieval Europe*, ed. Michael Jones (Gloucester, Alan Sutton, 1986), pp.61–80.
An article reviewing the evidence of motivations behind late medieval marriages and arguing that love could be an important factor.

Duckett, Eleanor, *Women and Their Letters in the Early Middle Ages* (Baltimore, Maryland, Barton-Gillet, 1965).
A published lecture surveying women's letters from Classical Rome to eighth-century England.

Ferrante, Joan M., *To the Glory of Her Sex: Women's Roles in the Composition of Medieval Texts* (Bloomington, Indiana, Indiana University Press, 1997).
An excellent study, which includes a chapter on women in medieval correspondence.

Finke, Laurie A., *Women's Writing in English: Medieval England* (London, Longman, 1999).
A broad survey of medieval women's writing that includes an excellent account of the epistolary genre, in addition to a section devoted to the Paston women, and dealing with questions of literacy, marriage, children, business, litigation, and style and storytelling.

Gies, Frances, and Josephine Gies, *A Medieval Family: The Pastons of Fifteenth-Century England* (New York, HarperCollins, 1998).
A chronological account of the family history. Illustrated. Intended for the general reader.

Harding, Wendy, 'Medieval Women's Unwritten Discourse on Motherhood: A Reading of Two Fifteenth-Century Texts', *Women's Studies* 21 (1992), pp.197–209.
A comparison of the treatment of the topics of pregnancy and giving birth in the Paston letters (especially those by Margaret Paston) and The Book of Margery Kempe.

Haskell, Ann S., 'The Paston Women on Marriage in Fifteenth-Century England', *Viator* 4 (1973), pp.459–71.
An article concentrating on the female perspective on marriage in the letters of the Paston women.

Knowles, David, 'The Religion of the Pastons', *Downside Review* 42 (1924), pp.143–63.
An old-fashioned but interesting account.

Krug, Rebecca, *Reading Families: Women's Literate Practice in Late Medieval England* (Ithaca, Cornell University Press, 2002).

A book length historical study examining the interaction between female literate practices, family relationships, and social circumstances. It focuses on Margaret Paston, Lady Margaret Beaufort, the Norwich Lollards, and the Bridgettine nuns of Syon Abbey.

Maddern, Philippa, 'Honour among the Pastons: Gender and Integrity in Fifteenth-Century English Provincial Society', *Journal of Medieval History* 14 (1988), pp.357–71.

A key study arguing that the Paston letters provide evidence that definitions of 'honour' in relation to battle, the law courts, the protection of family and friends, and personal integrity were extended to women.

O'Mara, V.M., 'Female Scribal Ability and Scribal Activity in Late Medieval England: The Evidence?', *Leeds Studies in English* 27 (1996), pp.87–130.

A much-needed study that, unfortunately, merely reiterates Norman Davis' assumptions and arguments in relation to the evidence of women's ability to write in the Paston letters.

Richardson, Malcolm, 'Women, Commerce, and Rhetoric in Medieval England' in *Listening to Their Voices: The Rhetorical Activities of Historical Women*, ed. Molly Meijer Wertheimer (Columbia, University of South Carolina Press, 1997), pp.133–49.

A discussion of the style of business letters by a selection of medieval women, including the Pastons, Stonors, and Plumptons.

Richmond, Colin, 'The Pastons Revisited: Marriage and Family in Fifteenth-Century England', *Bulletin of the Institute of Historical Research* 58 (1985), pp.25–36.

A self-explanatory account of love, negotiated alliances, engagements, and marriage.

Richmond, Colin, *The Paston Family in the Fifteenth Century: The First Phase* (Cambridge, Cambridge University Press, 1990).

The first volume in a trilogy that as whole comprises an exhaustive, but fascinating history of the family. Chapter 4 entitled 'Three Marriages' is of particular interest.

Richmond, Colin, *The Paston Family in the Fifteenth Century: Fastolf's Will* (Cambridge, Cambridge University Press, 1996).

The second volume in the trilogy. Chapter 6 on 'Money Matters' deals with Margaret's financial wrangles with her eldest son.

Richmond, Colin, *The Paston Family in the Fifteenth Century: Endings* (Manchester, Manchester University Press, 2000).

The last volume in the trilogy. Chapter 4 is devoted to Margaret Paston.

Richmond, Colin, 'Elizabeth Clere: Friend of the Pastons' in *Medieval Women: Texts and Contexts in Late Medieval Britain, Essays for Felicity Riddy*, ed. Jocelyn Wogan-Browne, Rosalynn Voaden, Arlyn Diamond,

Ann Hutchison, Carol M. Meale and Lesley Johnson (Turnhout, Brepols, 2000), pp.251–73.
An article providing biographical information about Elizabeth Clere and addressing the topic of female friendships, which has been hitherto overlooked in Paston scholarship.

Rosenthal, Joel T., 'Looking for Grandmother: The Pastons and their Counterparts in Late Medieval England' in *Medieval Mothering*, ed. John Carmi Parsons and Bonnie Wheeler (New York, Garland, 1996), pp.259–77.
An article addressing the neglected question of relationships between grandmothers and grandchildren, concentrating on Agnes and Margaret Paston.

Stiller, Nancy, *Eve's Orphans: Mothers and Daughters in Medieval English Literature* (Westport, Connecticut, Greenwood Press, 1980).
A book which includes a short discussion of mother-daughter relationships in the Paston letters.

Stoker, David, ' "Innumerable Letters of Good Consequence in History": The Discovery and First Publication of the Paston Letters', *The Library*, 6th series 17 (1995), pp.107–55.
A useful bibliographic account of how the letters came to be published and how they were received.

Tarvers, Josephine Koster, 'In a Woman's Hand? The Question of Medieval Women's Holograph Letters', *Post-Script* 13 (1996), pp.89–100.
A much-needed reassessment of the literacy of the Paston women.

Taylor, John, 'Letters and Letter Collections in England, 1300–1420', *Nottingham Medieval Studies* 24 (1980), pp.57–70.
A survey of the most important examples of the genre.

Thomsen, Lis Hygum, 'Agnes Paston' in *Female Power in the Middle Ages: Proceedings form the 2nd St Gertrud Symposium, Copenhagen, August 1986*, ed. Karen Glente and Lise Winther-Jensen (Copenhagen, C.A. Reitzel, 1989), pp.143–47.
A short biographical piece, praising Agnes' power and independence.

Watt, Diane, ' "No Writing for Writing's Sake": The Language of Service and Household Rhetoric in the Letters of the Paston Women' in *Dear Sister: Medieval Women and the Epistolary Genre*, ed. Karen Cherewatuk and Ulrike Wiethaus (Philadelphia, University of Pennsylvania Press, 1993), pp.122–38.
A reassessment of the Paston women, their literacy, education, epistolary style, and role in the household, focusing particularly on Margaret Paston.

Whitaker, Elaine E., 'Reading the Paston Letters Medically', *English Language Notes* 31 (1993), pp.19–27.

An article which discusses the roles of women as healers in the Paston letters in the context of changing attitudes to medicine.

Woolf, Virginia, 'The Pastons and Chaucer' in *The Common Reader*, 1ˢᵗ series (London, Hogarth Press, 1925), pp.13–38.

A romanticized, early feminist response to the Paston letters.

Glossary of Technical Terms

Arrears	Debts not paid by the date owed.
Assize	Periodical court held in the county to try civil and criminal cases.
Attornment	Acknowledgement of a new landlord.
Bailiff	Land steward or agent; chief official.
Close	Enclosure; enclosed field.
Distrain	To seize goods for debt.
Dower	Property settled on a wife by her husband at their marriage for her use after the husband's death.
Dowry	Property settled on a husband by his wife's family at their marriage: sometimes used for the dower or jointure.
Enfeoffed	Invested with a possession in fee.
Entailed	Limited in inheritance to certain heirs.
Fee	Ownership or inheritence, subject to feudal obligations; land held in fee.
Jointure	Dower.
Letters patent	Letters of privilege.
Manor	Estate consisting of the lord or owner's property and land and that let out to tenants.
Manorial court	Court held by the lord of the manor dealing with a variety of civil and criminal cases.
Ordinary	Judge acting by virtue of his office.
Receiver	Government official appointed to collect money due.
Relief	Fine paid to the overlord by the feudal tenant's heir on coming into possession of a property.
Rescue	Forcible release of a person or recovery of property.
Replevin	Writ of restitution; action to recover goods.
Sessions	Sittings of a court.

Sheriff	Royal shire official.
Shire	Administrative district.
Shire house	Hall where the business of the shire is conducted.
Soke	District under a particular jurisdiction.
Supersedeas	Writ to stop proceedings.

Index

Library of Medieval Women

Printed and bound by CPI Group (UK) Ltd, Croydon, CR0 4YY

13/04/2025

14656516-0003